The
of

CHRISTIAN & PAGAN
PRAYERS & PRACTICES
FOR EACH TURNING

The Celtic Wheel of the Year

CHRISTIAN & PAGAN
PRAYERS & PRACTICES
FOR EACH TURNING

COMPILED BY MEG LLEWELLYN

ANAMCHARA
BOOKS

ANAMCHARA BOOKS
Vestal, New York 13850
www.AnamcharaBooks.com

Paperback ISBN: 978-1-62524-518-2
Ebook ISBN: 978-1-62524-519-9

Modern prayers unless otherwise noted are by Meg Llewellyn.

Cover and interior design by Micaela Grace.

Cover illustration by Hildegard of Bingen.

Tree illustrations by Marina Bombina (Dreamstime.com).

CONTENTS

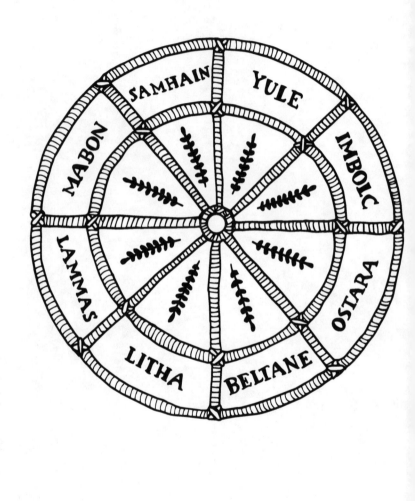

The Wheel of the Year in the Southern Hemisphere

Samhain	April 30/May 1
Winter Solstice (Yule)	June 21
Imbolc	August 1
Spring Equinox (Ostara)	September 21
Beltane	October 31
Summer Solstice	December 21
Lammas	February 2
Autumn Equinox (Mabon)	March 21

Introduction

Celtic spirituality is a term that's wide enough to cover many perspectives beneath its shelter, even while it means different things to different people. For some it's an ancient form of Christianity, one that's particularly appealing to modern followers of Jesus who want a faith that focuses on justice, tolerance, equality for women, creativity, and a love of Nature. For others, Celtic spirituality is a way to connect with a pre-Christian perspective on the world, one that celebrates the Earth and her seasons, finding deep spiritual meaning in land and sea and air. In either case, Celtic spirituality has it beginnings in history, but it has even deeper roots in our modern imagination. We believe that beneath it's shelter, we can find places of commonality between Christianity and Paganism, and so this book encompasses prayers and practices from both perspectives.

Like many other indigenous societies, Celtic society was structured and organized around the patterns of the Earth. People drew their sense of who they were, as well as their understanding of life's meaning, from their places within this structure. Today, our own society has structures that are just as firm—though we often barely notice them because they are part of the lens through which we see reality—but electricity, central heating, grocery stores, and mass transit have divorced us from the Earth's patterns. We observe the changing seasons, the repeating pattern of days and months and years, but from a distance. They lack the powerful intimacy and immediacy that they had for our ancestors.

The notion of time as a turning wheel played an important role in the Celts' societal structure. Today, our own concept of time, though very different from the Celts', is also an essential aspect of our society. We expect certain behaviors to be appropriate at certain ages of a person's life, and we measure individuals' places in society by the number of years they have lived. Summer brings with it a set of expectations for picnics and holidays and families traveling on vacations; autumn is the time when children go back to school and college semesters begin; winter focuses on the holidays with all their traditions, commercialization, and busyness. And yet there is often an element that is missing from all this, one that was essential to the Celts' understanding of the passing of time— the element of the spiritual, the connection to the Otherworld.

Societies need organization in order to function, and structures, of all sorts, serve a purpose. The Celts, however, recognized that these structures have meaning both at the ordinary, practical level and at far deeper depths. For the ancient Celts, time's cycle was truly a sacrament, a way to experience the sacred. Day and night, sun and moon, and the four seasons all carried profound spiritual messages.

Today, we often think of time as a straight line, an arrow that goes in one direction only, but more ancient cultures conceived of time as a turning circle. For the Celts, the wheel of time was divided into the four seasons, measured by solstices and equinoxes. These days were observed with rituals and celebrations that allowed human beings to experience their harmony with a larger, deeper, constantly turning world. Fertility, birth, growth, and death were repeating patterns that waxed and waned, and human beings consciously identified with these patterns, finding comfort and hope in their repetition.

The Celts' magic and ritual allowed them to participate in the spiritual world. They had a sense that they were working alongside the Divine to ensure that time's wheel was in good working order. As they collaborated with the Divine powers, they ensured that spring would follow winter, and harvest would follow spring.

Such thinking would likely be considered superstitious today—and yet the loss of our connection to the Earth's cycles has cost us. As we replaced our sharp awareness of sacred time with the time that is measured and standardized by clocks, we also learned to see Earth as a commodity there for our convenience. No longer did we thank God for each return of the sun; instead, we took for granted that human ingenuity and industry could ensure a constant stream of food and other products, regardless of the season of the year. This book is an opportunity to regain a little of that older, humbler sense of connection with the Earth, a chance to reexperience the Celts' wheel of the year overlain on our own calendars.

Prayers included here are both ancient and modern. As we read the prayers from long-ago folk who lived close to the agricultural cycles, we may at first find it difficult to relate to prayers concerning sheep and cattle, fields and fodder—but if we keep in mind that these things were the ordinary, workaday details of daily life, perhaps we can substitute our own meanings in their place. What are the details of our own work that concern us? What are the belongings for which we crave protection and blessing?

We have included here both the solstices and equinoxes, but also the Christian holidays that came to be identified with these or added to them. We have listed as well some of the more important Celtic saint days that fall in each month.

We have also included the Celtic tree calendar, adapting it as much as we can to our own twelve-month concept of the year. The original tree calendar, however, had thirteen lunar divisions. For convenience sake, we have forced these to correspond as closely as possible to the Gregorian calendar. This means that in order to keep on track, there are two "tree moons" during the month of May.

Each moon, each tree, had its own mythology and meaning. The Druids, the wise ones of ancient Celtic culture, are often credited with the creation of the tree calendar. This may or may not be true—or, equally likely, it may been made by Robert Graves, the twentieth-century Celtic researcher, poet, and author. Other students of ancient Celtic practice claim that the tree calendar is still more ancient, existing even before the Druids. If we can gain from this calendar a greater sense of time's depth and meaning, perhaps the historical details matter little.

Long, long before T. S. Eliot wrote similar words, Eriugena, the ninth-century Celtic theologian, wrote, "For the end of every movement is its beginning: that from which it was first moved, and to which it always longs to return, so there it may rest and be at peace." May the turning wheel of the year help you to find a sense of rest and peace, even amidst the chaos and catastrophe of our modern world.

—Meg Llewellyn

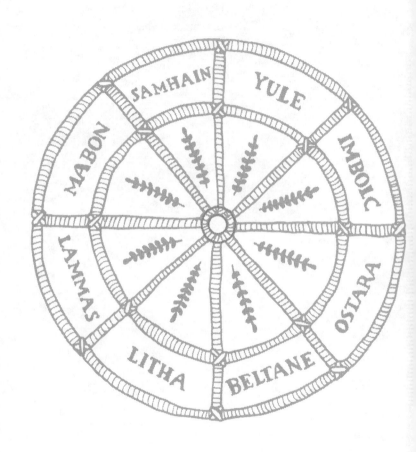

Every moment is born
from the death of the last moment.
Every spring is born from last year's autumn.
Every leaf that falls nourishes the new life
that will sprout when the earth is warmed again.
So why do we insist on clinging?
Why do we not let go as easily
as a tree lets go of both its leaves and its seeds,
letting one die so that the other will grow?

—*Angela Bailey*

The Reed Moon

Called **Negetal** (pronounced "nyettle") by the Celts, this is considered to be a time to go inward, celebrating the lives of our ancestors, while honoring the cycle of life and rebirth. Although not technically a tree, reeds played an essential role in early Celtic culture. Woven together, they provided the thatch for roofs; strewn underfoot, they were insulation against the mud and cold of the winter months; and so they are connected with protection and interconnection. Reeds are also used to make wind instruments, and their haunting strains connect us both to the breath of life and our sense of an Otherworld beyond this one.

Samhain and the Reed Moon

(NOVEMBER)

For the Celts, all "in-between" places and times are holy, whether they are the shores between land and water, the boundaries between political territories, bridges that cross streams of water, the twilight between day and night, or the transitions between the seasons. These liminal spaces, neither one thing nor another, are where human beings step outside their rigid mental boxes and catch a glimpse of Mystery. For the Celts, as well as for many modern Pagans, Samhain, as the juncture between the two halves of the year, is the most potent in-between time of all.

Samhain (pronounced "sow-in"), now celebrated on the first of November, is a cross-quarter day, located between the Autumn Equinox and the Winter Solstice. This is the Celtic end of the old year, the beginning of the new, and as such, it is a "hinge" in time, marking the transition between summer's light and winter's darkness. At the beginning of this period, the Celts believed, the gate between the worlds swings open, and it remains ajar until November 16, known as "Gate Closing," which coincides with the beginning of the Leonid Meteor Shower.

The season of Samhain, from late October into early November, cracked open the predictable order of time's cycle, letting people slip into a no-time space. This space of no-time belonged neither to the old year that had completed itself with the harvest, nor did it belong yet to the new year that began with winter. It was truly a crack between the two halves of the year, a time when all normal organization became inextricably entangled with the Otherworld's, making life unpredictable, frightening, and yet also filled with the potential for new discoveries, startling glimpses into the mystery of life. The past, present, and future became intertwined. The dead walked among the living, as did the faerie folk. It was a solemn time, but also a time of celebration, a festival of light to drive back the evil spirits, to affirm the power of life to endure the dark and cold of winter.

As normal time was abolished, so were traditional roles cast aside. Chaos reigned, and all sorts of antisocial pranks were considered acceptable. Boundaries between farms were no longer recognized, and so cattle were moved into different fields, and gates were pulled off their hinges and thrown into ditches. Well-fed children went begging at neighbors' doors. Men dressed as women, and women dressed as men.

The only celebration with which our modern Western world marks this season is Halloween, and we have retained the sense that this is a season of tricksters and disguise. But the Celtic Samhain is far more than a spooky children's holiday. This is the end of the old year's light and busyness, a time to prepare for the "womb-time" of winter, when we will turn inward, finding in the cold and darkness new possibilities, new potential for growth. The Celts understood that death and life are always joined.

At Samhain, the Celts honored and feasted their ancestors, not as the dead but as the living spirits of loved ones, the long line of kin who guarded the root-wisdom of the tribe. Samhain's Eve was the night to remember and toast these beloved ones, for the veil between the living and the dead was thought to be thin, and communication was possible. These Celtic celebrations in many ways resembled the Day of the Dead festivities celebrated by Mexican Americans and other Hispanic groups—not a somber festival but a celebration, a joyful acknowledgement that death is not the end of our family ties, that kinship survives even death. Our modern Halloween celebrations don't offer us that same connection with our ancestors.

Christianity and Western philosophy have often dismissed "ancestor worship" as either idolatry or delusion. Catholic Christians sometimes maintain a greater sense of connection with those who have left this life (and the November 1 celebration of All Saints Day is a time to acknowledge this), while Protestants generally perceive the dead as truly gone, existing in some eternal realm where any relationship with them must wait until we too leave this life. For those of us outside either of these spiritual traditions, the dead are largely irrelevant to our lives. We mourn those we have lost to death, and then we "move on," filling the holes they left as best we can. As for our ancestors, people we never personally knew, we generally regard them with curiosity rather than love.

The Celts, however, felt a sense of intimacy with their ancestors. They believed the Ancestors inhabited the Otherworld—not a faraway afterlife but a here-and-now that lies at a slant from our perceptions, a hidden landscape within the same world we see with our physical eyes, a place where the normal rules of time and space no longer exist. The portals to this world lie all around us in the "real world." Ritual connections with the Ancestors at Samhain not only strengthened family bonds but also heightened the Celts' awareness of this Otherworld and gave them greater perspective on the their own lives.

Free from the commercialization of Advent and New Year's, this is a private, holy time for many who celebrate the Wheel of the Year, a time to reflect on Nature's rhythms, on those we have loved who are no longer with us, on the battle against evil, on mysteries and magic, and on the meaning of time itself. During the Samhain season, perhaps we can remember that there is another reality that lies deeper than the measurements of clocks, calendars, and years, one that's wider and far less predictable than the grid of our calendars or the digital numerals on our cell phone clocks.

As we catch a glimpse of this reality, we step free—if only for a moment—from our careful definitions and boundary lines. In this no-time moment, we are free to scream and play like children on Halloween night, stripped naked of our usual roles, dancing in the darkness to the glimmer of candlelight in pumpkins. The normal world will return, with all its numbers and lines. But perhaps we will carry in our hearts something limitless and unfettered, a space of moonlight and magic where almost anything might be possible.

Samhain Ritual

A special harvest dinner is a typical way to celebrate Samhain. Set a place at the table for those who have passed into another life, people particularly close to you whom you want to honor and remember, as well as your visible guests, friends and family you've invited to share this occasion. Typical beverages include mulled wine, cider, and mead, which are shared with the Dead throughout the meal. Afterward, sit around an outdoor bonfire or an indoor fireplace, sharing memories and stories of those who are no longer with you in bodily form.

November also has the feast day of a Celtic saint—St. Winifred, whose day falls on the third of the month. Winifred is an Anglo-Saxon name that means reconciliation, protection, and peacemaking; in Welsh, her name was Gwenffrewi. She was a seventh-century woman from Wales who wandered alone for many years (according to some versions of the legend), while she recovered from the trauma of sexual assault. Legend tells that she wandered through the wilds of Wales, down into Devon, and from there across the channel into Europe, eventually reaching as far as Rome; when she finally returned from her travels, she was convinced that women could be more effective (not to mention safer) living in community. At the Synod of Winifred, she persuaded the Celtic church that vocations from God didn't necessarily need to be lived out in remote hermitages, as had been the practice. Winifred went on to build two convents and became the abbess of one of them. Today, she is considered the patron saint of those who have suffered sexual abuse.

SAMHAIN BLESSING I

From the Carmina Gadelica.

Power of raven be yours,
power of eagle be yours,
power of this day of power.

Power of storm be yours,
power of night be yours,
power of moon and star.

Power of sea be yours,
power of land be yours,
power of the heavens.

Goodness of sweet rest be yours,
goodness of the Earth be yours,
goodness of Heaven.

Each day be joyous,
no day be grievous,
honor and compassion.

Love of each face be yours,
soft death be yours,
your Savior's presence.

Each day be glad,
no day be sad,
life rich and full.

The strong help of the serpent be yours,
the strong help of fire be yours,
the strong help of grace.

The love-death of joy be yours,
the love-death of Mary be yours,
the loving arms of your Savior.

Yours be the might of rivers,
yours be the might of the ocean,
protection against specters and ghouls.

Yours be the might of home-fire,
yours be the might of strong rock,
the might of the Love on high.

Power of vision be yours,
power of heart's desire be yours,
power against all wandering spirits.

Power of surf be yours,
power of the bare branch be yours,
power of the cold.

The warmth of hearth be yours,
the warmth of sap in your bones,
the warmth of the Prince of heaven.

Voice of the swan be yours,
voice of honey be yours,
voice of the Son of the Stars.

The bounty of harvest be yours,
the bounty of heaven be yours,
your life whole and fruitful.

The loving grace of the Creator be yours,
the sweet grace of Christ be yours,
the gentle grace of the Spirit be yours,
washing you with grace,
shining you with light,
on this dark night.

SAMHAIN BLESSING II

A modern prayer.

Gateway between this world and spirit world;

thin night, dark night, night of spirits;

night to speak with those who have gone before.

A night to remember those who have gone before.

I honor you, those whose blood I carry.

I welcome you;

may your memory guide me into truth.

Watch over your kin who walk this Earth.

Protect us and guide us.

Your blood runs in my veins,

your spirit is in my heart,

your memories are in my soul;

bless us.

SAMHAIN BLESSING III

From the Carmina Gadelica.

May the cross of Christ be between me and the fays
that move hidden without and within.
May the cross of Christ be between me and all ill,
all ill will and ill mishap.
May the angels of heaven shield me,
the angels of heaven around me this night,
soul and body alike.
Christ's circling around me,
guarding from every specter and evil,
from every power in the darkness,
every power to hurt.
Christ's strong circling
keeping me from all ruin
that creeps toward me this night.

SAMHAIN PRAYER I

A modern prayer.

Great One, God of life and love,
as we stand at the edge of winter,
our fields are bare and empty;
the trees stand sleeping;
our hearts turn inward,
and the world's fabric grows thin.
We feel the souls of those who have crossed over,
brushing past us in the air.
May their way be blessed
as they travel to the Summerlands.
Remind us that what seems now to be ending,
is only the beginning of something new,
though it lies outside our sight.
The seed must die,
the earth must sleep,
and trees must stand bare and silent,
before new life can come.
We too must die before we can be reborn.
This day of darkness is but the dawn
of something new.

SAMHAIN PRAYER II

A modern prayer.

Lord of Life,
my heart is quiet, dark,
standing in the shadow of winter's cold,
of days of long darkness.
Lord of Life,
You seem to be asleep.
Have You left me here
alone in the shadow of winter's night?
But, no, I hear You whisper.
You have not gone,
but I have gone
into the great womb,
a time of rest, of darkness,
of possibility yet unborn.
Here in the darkness,
the spark of light still burns,
waiting for the spring.

Though You seem absent,
though all is dark,
this is the time of new seeing,
inner seeing,
visions of the unknown,
and glimpses of God yet unguessed.
My soul is hidden from my sight,
but not from Yours, O great God,
Mother of Darkness and Father of Light.
I sleep, I dream, waiting for the spring,
trusting that You will keep my life alive,
You will keep my light alive,
through dark and cold and bitter night.
This is but the veil
that for a moment hides
Your burning heart.

THANKSGIVING AT SAMHAIN

A modern prayer by William Palmer.

Lord of the changing seasons,
of harvest time, frost, and hearth fire,
I thank You for this holy time of the turning year.
A hard freeze this All Saint's Day morning.
The russet leaves fall thickly in the still, early light.
Like all the men and women who have ever lived,
they return to the Earth.
I thank You, Lord, for this moment in time,
this moment of clear revelation.
I thank You for the faith of my ancestors, remembered this day,
for Halloween candy, and pumpkin pie,
and the Communion of Saints,
for cozy evenings
and the low-angled sun of a November afternoon.
In the name of the dead, I thank You!
In the name of the living, I thank You!
In the name of those to come, I thank You!

PRAYER OF THE REED MOON

A modern prayer.

Moon of the coming darkness,
your cold winds wail over the marshes,
stirring the dry reeds, making them whisper
messages of the coming winter.
Dark Lady, bless me in your darkness.
Take that in me that needs to rest in the dark,
all that needs to wait, to slow, to cease.
May I not resist your hand.
Teach me to be still,
so that the Lord of Life and Light
can transform me in the dark.

PRAYER TO ST. WINIFRED

A modern prayer.

Blessed Winifred,
holy peacemaker,
shaper of reconciliation,
loving protector,
we ask that you grant healing,
to each of us who have been severed
from our sense of our own identity.
Heal those who bear the scars
of violence and violation.
Make us intact once more,
whole and holy,
able to labor in your footsteps,
bringing peace, reconciliation,
and protection
to all who are vulnerable,
to all who have been broken,
to all who have been violated.
Help us to heal together
in your blessed name.

The Elder Moon

Called **Ruish** by the Celts (pronounced "roo-esh"), the Elder Moon is a time of endings and new beginnings. Elder is said to protect against demons and other negative forces—including visible ones, like flies, mosquitos, and other pests—which is why branches were hung over doors and windows. Associated with the banishment of negative qualities, the tree also has actively positive attributes; its bark, flowers, and berries all have medicinal qualities and have been used for centuries in folk medicine to treat a variety of ailments. Modern scientists have found that the tree has antiviral properties. Although the elder tree can be damaged easily, it recovers quickly and springs back to life, representing the rejuvenation of life at the time of the Winter Solstice, a time of beginnings and endings, births and deaths.

The Winter Solstice, Yule, and the Elder Moon

(DECEMBER)

In the Northern Hemisphere at this time, we experience the longest nights of the year and the shortest days. As we more consciously link our awareness to the wheel of the year, our understanding of our own personal growth cycles may also deepen. This is a sacred time of rest and reflection before the awakening toward brighter days. It is a time to experience the fruitfulness of darkness, to wait in silence and unknowing for new inspirations to emerge. As Carl Jung taught, when we explore our own darkness, we open ourselves to an essential source of our own personal power. The darkness can become a spiritual cradle into which new light and life is born.

The Winter Solstice, coming as it does just as nights are longest and coldest, marks the return of light. Winter still has many long months to go, but from now on, the days will grow longer and the nights shorter. Earlier cultures may have feared that winter might never end, that life might never return to the Earth, but the Winter Solstice brings the promise of hope. Darkness is a necessary part of life, but one day the light always returns.

Ancient people understood the sun's return as a sacramental moment. At the Newgrange tomb in Ireland, for a few days around the Winter Solstice the tomb's dark interior is lit with sunlight streaming down the passageway. Newgrange was constructed in such a way to align precisely with the winter sun, creating a meeting place for Heaven and Earth, after which the sun would grow ever stronger. This natural ritual demonstrated the ever-renewed bond between the sun and the Earth, an annual covenant that that for one more year the Sun would be reborn and the light would return in full strength; the Earth would grow warm again, plants would return from the dead, and the crops would grow. Life would continue.

Celtic oral traditions indicate that the tomb at Newgrange was associated with not only death but also with birth. At the Winter Solstice, when the Sun enters the passage and chamber at dawn, it is a moment of conception. The days that follow are the fruit of this union. Life has been reborn.

Newgrange is also said to have been the place where the great mythical hero Cúchulainn was conceived. His spiritual father, Lugh, visited his mother in a dream while she was staying at Newgrange. Lugh's name comes from an ancient root word that meant "flashing light," and so Cúchulainn is the son of light, conceived at the time of the Winter Solstice.

In the fourth century, when the Church set the observation of Jesus' birth at the time of the Winter Solstice, it made sense to the Pagan world. Here was another Divine Hero, the Son of Light; when else would he be born except at the time of the Sun's return to the Earth? For the people in Norse and Celtic lands, the ancient holiday referred to as Yule merged with the Nativity of Christ. One overlay the other, a comfortable fit between ancient and new understandings of the spiritual realm.

Winter Solstice Ritual

There are many Yule rituals that are probably a part of your Christmas customs: decorating with evergreen and lights, for example, and gift-giving. You might deepen your understanding of the season by honoring the night of the Winter Solstice, December 22, as a festival of light. Host a special meal with friends and family, and before eating, sit for a few moments in darkness, with no lights lit. Think of the things that have died in your life. Ponder what is wanting to be born, what new inspirations and ideas are coming to life. Then, one by one, light as many candles as you can gather, and eat your meal by their light, celebrating the birth of Light.

AN ADVENT PRAYER

A modern prayer by William Palmer.

Lord of the shortening day,

of the snowflake, the fir tree, and the ice-rimmed lake,

be with me in the dark and cold of these four weeks.

The Faith of the prophets who foretold

His coming to a waiting world,

be the Faith in me!

The Hope of the holy men and women who longed for

His coming,

be the Hope in me!

The Love of His gentle mother

to whom He came in such humility,

be the Love in me!

In Faith, in Hope, in Love,

through these short, cold days of the early winter,

sustain me, O God, as I await Your coming!

WINTER SOLSTICE PRAYER

A modern prayer.

My heart lies dormant,
dark and cold like the earth beneath the soil.
Frozen clods cling to my very being,
my deepest sense of my self,
and yet I feel on my face the returning sun.
The Earth's heartbeat is steady,
even in the cold and dark,
confident in the promise of the Spring.
Keep me steady too, bright Spirit of Light,
even in the cold and dark.

PRAYER TO MOTHER WINTER

A modern prayer.

O mighty Winter, Mother clothed in ice,
watch over us, cover us with your cold blanket,
keep us safe as we sleep beneath the snow.
Guard our dreams; keep life alive
within our cold hearts.
Frost on the world, and on our souls,
we huddle next to home fires,
waiting for the Light.
Hold out your arms, Mother Winter.
Welcome back the Light.

WINTER HAIL

Adapted from an ancient prayer.

Hail to the Christ King,

blessed is He,

who came to us in the dark and cold.

Blessed be the house and all therein.

Find His blessing on your cupboards.

Find His blessing in your barrels.

Find His blessing in the beams of your house.

Hail to the Christ King,

blessed is He,

who came to us in the dark and cold.

Let God be armor and clothing.

Let God be warmth in winter cold;

let God be health when ills lurk near.

God's blessings last around your house.

Healthy around the hearth and table be you all.

May the foundations of your house stand firm

against the winter wind,

and may all who dwell therein be firm as well.

Prosperity be upon this dwelling,

on floor and walls, on rafters, wood, and stone.

Deliver it to God from cellar to roof.

Hail to the Christ King,

blessed is He,

who came to us in the dark and cold.

Why sorrow in the cold? Why tremble in the dark?

The soles of the King's feet have touched the Earth.

His Light has illumined the land.

His Light shines from the Earth, shines from the stars.

The plains glow to Him, the mountains glow to Him.

Soil and sea are illumined.

God the Lord of Heaven has opened a Door.

Christ of hope, Door of joy, Golden Sun in winter dark.

Hail to the Christ King,

blessed is He,

who came to us in the dark and cold.

In time of change and fear,

He is everlasting,

Without beginning, without end,

for all ages, all time,

into the time beyond time.

Offer to the Being all your home;

include each stick, each stone, each rod and cloth.

Offer again all that you have,

and let there be joy.

Ho! Hail! Blessed is the King of Being!

From everlasting to eternity, Being without end.

Hail to the Christ King,

blessed is He,

who came to us in the dark and cold.

HEY THE GIFT IN WINTERTIME

Adapted from the Carmina Gadelica.

Hey the Gift, ho the Gift
that came to us in winter.
See the hills, see the host on wing, see the icy strand;
Christ the King of Glory
was born of human flesh.
See angels in the clouds, see messengers in the snow,
coming with speech and friendship for all humankind.

The Child of the dawn is born, Child of the clouds,
Child of the planet, Child of the stars,
Child of the rain, Child of the dew,
Child of the heavens, Child of the sky,
Child of the flame, Child of the dark,
Child of all spheres, Child of the moon,
Child of the elements, Child of the sun.
Child of God-Mind and Mary.
Christ is the first of all news, the best of all news.
Hey the Gift, ho the Gift
that came to us in winter.

WINTER POWER

Adapted from an ancient prayer.

I am the Winter Gift,
I am the Power,
I am the Poor,
I am the Man of Winter,
the Man of Cold and Night.
I am the Son of Woman and God-Mind.
Open the door, and I am there.
See the winter birds,
bringing kindness and friendship.
See me in winter cold.
Open the door, and I am there,
bringing kindness and friendship and power.

WINTER PRAYER FOR THE STRANGER

Adapted from an ancient prayer.

The foam-white Beloved came to us
without one home in all the world.
Tender and holy, He was driven into the cold.
Immanuel! A Stranger!
You angels of power,
come down, come down!
Greet us! Show us!
Show us Christ in the stranger.
You Three of Power, kiss the cold stranger.
Hold his hand.
Warm his feet with the hair on your heads.
O! World-Pervading One! O Jesu! O Mary!
O Angels Three—Michael, Gabriel, and Raphael!
Do not forsake the stranger to the winter cold.

CHRISTMAS EVE CAROL

From the Carmina Gadelica.

This night is the long night.
It will snow and it will drift;
white snow there will be till day;
White moon there will be till morn.
This night is the eve of the Great Nativity;
this night is born the Virgin's son;
this night is born Jesus, Son of glory;
this night is born to us the root of our joy.

This night gleamed the sun on the mountains high;
this night gleamed sea and shore together;
this night was born Christ the King of greatness.
Before we heard that the Glory was come,
we heard the wave upon the strand;
before we heard His foot had reached the Earth,
we heard the song of the angels.
This night is the long night,
when wood and tree glow to Him,
when mount and sea glow to Him,
when land and plain glow to Him,
when His foot came down to Earth.

CHRISTMAS CAROL

From the Carmina Gadelica.

This night is the eve of the great Nativity,
born is the Son of Mary the Virgin,
the soles of His feet have reached the earth,
the Son of Glory down from on high.
Heaven and earth glowed to Him.
All hail! Let there be joy!
The peace of earth to Him, the joy of heaven to Him,
behold His feet have reached the world;
the homage of a King be His, the welcome of a Lamb be His,
King all victorious, Lamb all glorious,
earth and ocean illumined to Him,
All hail! Let there be joy!

The mountains glowed to Him, the plains shown to Him,
the voice of the waves with the song of the strand,
announcing to us that Christ is born,
Son of the King of kings from the land of salvation;
shone the sun on the mountains high to Him,
all hail! Let there be joy!

Shone to Him the Earth and Sphere together,
God the Lord has opened a Door;
Son of Mary Virgin, hasten to help me,
O Christ of hope, O Door of joy,
Golden Sun of hill and mountain,
All hail! Let there be joy!

THE ANIMALS' PRAYER

Adapted from an ancient prayer.

"Christ is born!" crowed the cock.

"When?" croaked the raven.

"This night," cawed the crow.

"Where?" asked the ox.

"Bethlehem," said the cow.

"Let us go," said the donkey.

"Let us go!" said my heart.

CHRISTMAS MORNING PRAYER

Adapted from an ancient prayer.

Hark! No angel song we hear,
but yet listen! The bees awake
and hum their song of praise.
Bird and beast join in.
Christ is born!
Christ is born!
Light has risen within the dark.
Light has risen from the dark.

PRAYER TO THE SUN GOD

A modern prayer.

Wheel of Fire, Eye of the Sky,

I honor you on this,

the shortest day of the year.

Your light is shortened, but undimmed.

Even in these darkest times,

you are the beacon who lights our way

to the promise of the future

Welcome, Wheel of Fire, great Eye of the Sky!

Return to us.

Bring life back to Earth.

Bring light back to your children.

Hail bright Wheel! Hail great Eye!

Welcome!

YULE PRAYER

Traditional Yule charm.

May the log burn,
may the wheel turn,
may evil spurn,
till the sun return.

YULE WELCOME

From an ancient prayer borrowed from the Norse.

Beneath the tree of light and life,

a blessing at this season of Yule

to all that sit at my hearth.

Today we are brothers and sisters,

we are family,

and I drink to our health!

Today we do not fight;

we bear no one ill will.

Today is a day to offer hospitality

to all that cross my threshold

in the name of the season.

YULE BLESSING

Modern prayer of gratitude.

I am grateful, Spirit of Light,
for all I have been given.
And yet I sorrow, Spirit of the Fire,
for all that I have not.
Remind me that if I have less than some,
I have more than others,
and regardless, I am blessed.

I am grateful for my family,
for the people who love me.
I am grateful for my home,
for the walls that shelter me.
I am grateful for my friends,
those who understand me.
I am grateful for my enemies,
those who challenge me.
I am grateful for the animals
who surround me with their small lives.
I am grateful for the Earth,
who gives me life.
I am grateful for the Spirit,
who gives me joy.

PRAYER OF THE ELDER MOON

A modern prayer.

Old woman of the night,
we ask that you bless us in the darkness.
You who has seen countless endings,
eternal beginnings,
the never-ending circle of light and dark,
remind us that the Day Star has been born.
This is the birth month of the Light.

The Birch Moon

*The Celtic name for this month is **Beth** (pronounced "beh"). The nights governed by the Birch Moon are considered to be a time of rebirth and regeneration as we look toward the light once more. When a forested area burns, birch is the first tree to grow back, and when the great glaciers of the last ice age receded, birch trees would have been some of the first plant life to recolonize the ice-scoured land. As a result, the birch has come to symbolize the renewal that is appropriate as well for the month after the Winter Solstice. According to Celtic mythology, birch was also good for purification from evil, and birch broomsticks were considered to be the most effective for cleaning, while birch twigs were hung over cradles to protect babies.*

Hogmanay and the Birch Moon

(JANUARY)

Although the Celts considered Samhain to be the beginning of the new year, New Year's Eve at the start of January is celebrated around the world. The Celts also have a long heritage associated with this event, and the Scottish Celts even have their own name for it—Hogmanay.

Scholars of Scottish history and culture have several theories about where the word came from. Scotland is near to the Norse countries, and over the years, in both friendship and war, the Norse cast their influence of the land to their south—and the Norse word for the Yule feast was "Hoggo-nott." The Flemish words *hoog min dag,* meaning "great love day," may have also played a role, as may the Anglo Saxon *haleg monath,* "holy month," the Gaelic *oge maidne,* "new morning," or the French *homme est né,* "man is born." Perhaps several of these words blended together to become "Hogmanay."

Regardless of the source of the word, many of the traditional Hogmanay celebrations may have originally been brought to Scotland by the invading Vikings of the eighth and ninth centuries. When the stiff-laced Protestants put an end to Christmas celebrations in the seventeenth century, condemning it as a "popish" festival, Hogmanay survived through the centuries. Up until the middle of the twentieth century, many Scots worked over Christmas and then celebrated their winter solstice holiday at the New Year.

Family and friends gathered to celebrate the event with feasting and gifts. First, however, before the celebration at midnight, the house should be cleaned (or "redded") and the old ashes emptied out of the fireplace. All debts should be cleared and arguments forgiven, so that the New Year could be welcomed without any old ties to the past.

"First footing" is a common element of the celebration. To ensure good luck for the household, the first foot across the threshold of the house should be a dark-haired male (someone who looked as little like a Viking invader as possible!), bringing with him pieces of coal, shortbread, salt, a black bun, and a little whisky.

Today's Hogmanay celebrations also include fireworks and torchlight processions through the streets of Scottish cities and towns. One of the most spectacular fire ceremonies takes place in Stonehaven, south of Aberdeen on Scotland's northeast coast. Giant fireballs swing on long metal poles, each requiring many men to carry them as they are paraded up and down the High Street. The swinging balls of fire signify the power of the sun, renewing and purifying the world.

Hogmanay Ritual

This is a night for partying with friends and family—but before the festivities begin, take a few quiet moments to consider what is tying you to the past. What is holding you back, keeping you bound, preventing you from growing or exploring new paths? Write on a piece of paper whatever comes to mind—and then consciously let it go. Burn the piece of paper.

Other Celtic holy days fall during January. The first of these is the feast day of St. Ita on January 15. Ita was a sixth-century Irish woman who founded a school and convent at Killeedy, which still bears her name; a holy well still marks the site of her church. She is sometimes referred to as the "foster mother of the saints," for her school was a training ground for many of the boys who went on to become spiritual leaders, including St. Brendan. Many people sought her out for her wise counsel, as well as her medicinal skills. She once told St. Brendan, "The three things most displeasing to God are: a mouth full of hate, a heart full of resentment, and trusting in material wealth. The three things most pleasing to God are: the firm belief of a pure heart in God, the simple spiritual life, and generosity to others."

A century before Ita, another spiritual woman, Dwynwen, lived in Wales. According to legend, Dwynwen was forbidden to marry the man she loved, and instead, her father arranged for her to be married to a different man. Dwynwen was so upset that she prayed God would make her forget her lover. An angel gave her a potion to erase his memory and turned the man into a block of ice. God then gave three wishes to Dwynwen. Her first wish was that her lover be thawed and restored to life; her second was that God would meet the hopes and dreams of all true lovers; and the third was that she never be forced into marriage against her will. Dwynwen then devoted herself to God's service for the rest of her life. She founded a convent off the coast of Anglesey, where the ruins of the church still stand. Her feast day on January 25 is celebrated by lovers, a Celtic Valentine's Day, and she is believed to intercede on behalf of the broken hearted.

NEW YEAR'S PRAYER TO MARY

Adapted from an ancient prayer.

O Mary! Bless our cupboards bare.

Give us food in winter leanness.

May our storehouses keep us till spring's new growth.

Nourish us when we are cold and hungry.

When there is nothing left,

be our mother.

You are brighter than the moon rising over the hillside.

You are brighter than the summer sun.

You are fuller than the flooded river.

The bard cannot tarry in the cold,

so give us now your blessing,

before he leaves us cold and silent.

May we give your blessing to another,

knowing you will be our mother

when there is nothing left.

The Son stands at the threshold of the New Year.

Open the door for your Son.

Let Him come in.

HOGMANAY CAROL

From an ancient song.

I am now come to your country,

to renew the year.

I will come over the door lintel.

I will climb your steps.

I will sing My song so you can hear Me,

slowly, purposefully, mindfully.

I will bless your storehouses, your animals, your kin.

I carry the New Year blessings in My pocket.

It is like a small gift of summer's bloom.

I am at the door.

Get up and let Me in.

BLESSING THE NEW YEAR I

From the Carmina Gadelica.

God, bless to me the new day of the new year,
never vouchsafed to me before;
You have given me this time, O God,
to bless Your own Presence.
Bless to me my eyes;
may my eyes bless all they see.
I will bless my neighbor;
may my neighbor bless me.
God, give me a clean heart for this clean year.
Do not lose sight of me in the days to come.
Bless all I love,
bless children, friends, and lovers;
my animals, my daily work.
Bless my wealth, whether meager or large.
Give me strength to give all to You.

BLESSING THE NEW YEAR II

A modern prayer.

King of moon and sun,
King of stars beloved,
You know our need,
for You are the merciful God of life.
Each day in this new year,
remind us that we only move
because Your Spirit breathes in us.

Each day in this new year, when we awake,
turn our thoughts to the King of hosts Who loves us.
Be with us through each day.
Be with us through each night;
be with us each night and day.
Be with us each day and night.
Be with us through each full moon and each dark moon.
Be with us through sun and storm.
Be with us while the year turns round again.

PRAYER FOR THE BIRCH MOON

A modern prayer.

Hail, new moon of the new year,
fair guide of the sky,
fair one of grace,
loved one of my heart,
dear one of the heavens,
bring new life.
Bring beginnings.
Bring life from death,
and light from dark.
Hail, Lady, new moon of the new year.

As the birch ventures into the burned field,
Lady, fill my life with new life, new growth,
springing up from the ashes.
Hail, new moon of the new year,
white-limbed lady,
give us your blessing.

BIRCH MONTH PRAYER

A modern prayer.

In this quiet time,
time of cold and dark and sleep,
may light conceive new life in me.
In this dark time,
time of rest and silence,
grow light in me,
in the darkness of my heart.
In this empty time,
time of loneliness and ice,
keep life alive in me.
Let me rest, knowing life waits.
Let me ponder, knowing light has come.
Let me sleep, and send new dreams
to light my darkness.
May I be like the birch,
standing silent in the snow,
my bark as white as moonlight,
my roots asleep in the cold earth,
waiting for the spring.

PRAYER FOR WINTER COLD

Adapted from the Carmina Gadelica.

As ice covers hill and pasture,
keep Your own warmth, O God,
around my house and barns.
Even as I clothe my body with wool.
cover my soul with the shadow of Your wing.
Do not forget me and mine
when winter storms moan in the night,
and may my heart never grow so cold
that I forget You, O God of light and glory.

THE BLESSING OF
THE HEARTH IN WINTER

Adapted from an ancient Welsh blessing.

Flame, slender, curved, blue and gold,

leaping from the peat and wood,

give breath and heat and life through the cold night.

Be a steady burning, gentle and generous.

Quicken my heart's roots in winter cold.

Fire, fragrant, fair, and peaceful,

cause no grief nor havoc in our home.

Heat, warm my child and all I love

who gather around you now,

in the name of Christ who rules the winter,

who gave us corn and bread and blessing enough;

in the name of Christ who rules the cold,

who gave us corn and bread and blessing enough

to last us through the winter.

WINTER PRAYER

Adapted from the Carmina Gadelica.

Holy Creator of truth,
kind Creator of mercy,
deliver me from the cold and ice,
deliver me from all evil spells,
deliver me from the charms that would work ill
in my flesh or in my family or in the animals in my care.
Draw Your blessing over this winter day,
draw Your own cross over this winter day,
and on every day;
draw Your cross on my heart this winter night,
and on every night.

PRAYER TO ST. ITA

A modern prayer.

Blessed Ita,
who thirsted for God,
may we, like you
be thirsty for the Bright God,
the Giver of Life.
Take hate from our mouths,
remove resentment from our hearts,
and remind us not place our trust
in the things we can see and touch,
nor in wealth and riches,
but only in the love of the Bright God,
the Giver of All.
Help us to please the Life-Giver
with a firm trust and pure heart.
Teach us to live simply.
Remind us to give generously.
Make us thirsty for God.

PRAYER TO ST. DWYNWEN

A modern prayer.

Sweet Dwynwen,
you knew both the joy
and the pain of love.
We pray for all whose hearts are broken.
We pray for all who love happily and securely.
We pray for lovers to have the strength
to love long and well.
Comfort those who sorrow for a lost love.
Give clarity to those who are confused.
Give depth to those who celebrate love's rewards.
In your name, may we always choose love.
In your name and in the name of Christ,
his mother Mary, and Blessed Joseph,
may we, like you,
work always to build the house of love.

The Rowan Moon

The Rowan Moon is a time of protection against evil. Known by the Celts as **Luis** *(pronounced "loush"), the tree's red berries were thought to guard against dangerous enchantment. An old rhyme stated, "Rowan tree and red thread make the witches lose their speed." Sprigs of rowan were used to guard cattle and dairies from disease and mischief, and across Celtic lands, crosses made from rowan twigs and tied together with red threads were carried in pockets, sewed into the lining of coats, or hung over the lintels of the house. The red berries were also associated with flame and with Brigid, saint and goddess of the fire.*

Imbolc and the Rowan Moon

(FEBRUARY)

Imbolc is a cross-quarter day, the halfway point between the Winter Solstice and the Summer Solstice. Traditionally, it begins at sundown on February 1, and continues through February 2 (what North America celebrates as Ground Hog's Day). This is the earliest breath of spring, the first glimpses of new life as we turn our attention to winter's end. In some areas of the northern hemisphere, the earliest spring flowers may appear now, while others may still be blanketed with snow.

The word *imbolc* means "in the belly of the mother," for this is the time of pregnancy and the stirring of new life in seeds and creatures. Another name for this day is *Oimelc*, which means "milk of ewes," for this was also lambing season in the Celtic world. In ancient times, the birth of lambs would bring a ready supply of milk to feed the tribe through the rest of the late winter and spring, until the land could again provide sustenance.

This day is especially sacred to Brigid, the saint and the goddess, the patron of healing and the hearth, smithcraft and poetry. At Imbolc, the Celts honored Brigid's role as protector of hearth and home—of the fires that light our way through the dark times of winter—as well her role as a fertility goddess. Brigid, both the saint and the goddess, was said to inhabit liminal spaces, the thresholds between light and dark, time and space, and so this day, the doorway between winter and spring, was a time to celebrate Brigid's blessings.

The snowdrop flower is one of the first to appear after winter, in some regions poking up through the snow right about the beginning of February—and according to legend, Brigid walks across the land, strewing snowdrops from her mantle. Then, as spring progresses, she flings out her mantle and turns the world green.

Since Brigid is a goddess of fire—the fire of the hearth, the fire of the forge, and the fire of inspiration—many modern Imbolc traditions involve flame. In Britain, fire festivals with Morris dancers often commemorate her day, an ancient tradition that stretches back into the mists of time. Brigid's crosses are woven together from wheat stalks and exchanged as symbols of protection and prosperity for the coming year. Hearth fires are put out and relit, and a broom is placed by the front door to symbolize sweeping out the old and welcoming the new. Candles are lit and placed in each room of the house to honor Brigid's flame.

Another celebration of the day includes a young girl who is chosen to be a representative of Brigid by carrying candles or wearing them on her head. She symbolizes the light and life brought by Brigid back to the earth. The Church gave this ancient holy day the name of Candlemas, a day to make and bless a year's worth of candles to light the coming year. It was also the commemoration of the infant Jesus' presentation in the

Temple—the revelation of the Light of the World, still a baby but growing, just as the spark of Candlemas swells into the full flame of summer.

Spiritually, this is a time to consider that which has been hibernating within you. During winter's long months of cold, what has been sleeping, waiting to emerge, transformed, into the light? Pay attention to the stirrings of new life. What do you feel changing in your life and within you? Where are the transitions to something new occurring? Like the groundhog that pokes his head out of the earth, now is the time for you to look out from the darkness of your own inner depths. The time is coming soon for you to emerge, but for now, anticipate what lies ahead. Make plans for the coming spring, both physically and spiritually. Despite the discomfort of venturing outside your comfort zones, embrace this time of new beginnings.

St. Brigid's Day Ritual

A Brigid's Bed (sometimes also called a Breed's Bed or a Bride's Bed) is a little bed made for Brigid, set by the hearth or the doorway to welcome her to come in out of the cold for the night. It could be a doll's bed made up with blankets, or it might be simply a blanket, representing Brigid's mantle. Little gifts and treats—symbolizing Brigid's blessings of springtime—are then left in the bed, for the children (or the young at heart) of the household to find in the morning.

PRAYER TO SAINT BRIGID AT THE END OF WINTER

Based on an ancient prayer.

Radiant flame of gold, sweet foster-mother of Christ,
I call your name.
Let not death come to my house at winter's end.
Let us not be harried and hungry.
You will not let me be put into a cell.
You will not let me be wounded.
You will not let me fall into forgetfulness of Christ.
You are my gentle foster-mother.
You bring new life at winter's end.
I am sick in my heart;
winter lingers in my bones.
As you did help bring Jesus from Mary's womb,
bring new life from me.
I am winter-bare, without gold or corn or cows.
Aid me, O Brigid! Great is my winter need.
Bring springtime to the land.
Bring springtime to my heart.

BRIGID'S DAY BLESSING I

From the Carmina Gadelica.

Brigid of the mantle,
Brigid of the peat,
Brigid of the curling hair,
Brigid of prophecy.
Brigid of the white feet,
Brigid of calmness,
Brigid of the white palms,
Brigid of the cattle.
Brigid, woman-friend,
Brigid, woman-helper,
Brigid, fire-keeper,
Brigid, gentle woman.
Brigid, Mary's tresses,
Brigid, Nurse of Christ—
I call on you, on your day of blessing,
at winter's end, and spring's new beginning.

I shall not be slain,
I shall not be wounded,
I shall not be put in a cell,
I shall not be broken,
I shall not be torn asunder,
I shall not be diminished,
I shall not be downtrodden,
I shall not be stripped bare,
I shall not be torn,
nor will Christ abandon me
or leave me forgotten.
As winter ends and spring begins,
let not sun burn me,
let not fire burn me,
let no ray of light burn me,
let no moon blanch me.

Give me your blessing, bright Brigid,
that no river drown me,
no salt water drown me,
no winter flood drown me,
no spring torrent drown me.
Give me your springtime blessing,
that no nightmare shall lie on me,
no black sleep shall lie on me,
no crawling thing shall find me.

I am under Mary's keeping,
and you, bright Brigid,
are my beloved companion.
You are my comrade-woman,
you are my maker of song,
you are my helper,
you are my woman of guidance,
you guide me to my heart's desire,
to my heart's desire,
at winter's end and spring's beginning.

BRIGID'S DAY BLESSING II

A modern prayer by Lilly Weichberger.

On Brigid's Day,
may the bright Goddess's presence
bring you comfort and peace;
may her flame warm your heart and hearth;
may her bright fires inspire
your thoughts, words, and deeds.
May you be forged by your trials
and her strong hand
into your most perfect self.
May her cool water
heal and sooth your sorrows.
May her mantle protect you from all harm,
and her presence be a light
to guide you through the darkness,
now and always.
Blessed be.

PRAYER TO BRIGID I

From the Carmina Gadelica.

Brigid of the Mantle, encompass us,
Lady of the Lambs, protect us,
Keeper of the Hearth, kindle us.
Beneath your mantle, gather us,
and restore us to memory.
Mothers of our mother,
foremothers strong,
guide our hands in yours;
remind us how to kindle the hearth.
To keep it bright, to preserve the flame.
Your hands upon ours,
our hands within yours,
to kindle the light,
both day and night.
The Mantle of Brigid about us,
the Memory of Brigid within us,
the Protection of Brigid keeping us
from harm, from ignorance,
from heartlessness.
This day and night,
from dawn till dark,
from dark till dawn.

PRAYER TO BRIGID II

Modern prayer by Kenneth McIntosh.

Saint Brigid,

you were a woman of peace.

You brought harmony where there was conflict.

You brought light to the darkness.

You brought hope to the downcast.

May the mantle of your peace cover

those who are troubled and anxious,

and may peace be firmly rooted in our hearts

and in our world, on this your holy day.

Inspire us to act justly

and to reverence all God has made.

Brigid, you were a voice

for the wounded and the weary.

Strengthen what is weak within us.

Calm us into a quietness that heals and listens.

May we grow this day, and each day

into greater wholeness

in mind, body and spirit.

IMBOLC BLESSING

From the Carmina Gadelica.

The joy of lambs be yours,
the joy of new life be yours,
the joy of the coming of the light,
the joy of God on your face,
the circle of God around your head,
Brigid's light in your home.

AT IMBOLC

Modern prayer by William Palmer.

I thank You, Lord, for the wisdom of the ancestors,

Who marked the coming of spring in bleak February.

For shining-bright Brigid!

For Candlemas Day, when tradition tells us to be sure to have

half our wood and half our hay.

For the groundhog lumbering out of his den.

For the lengthening day and the higher-arcing sun.

For the drip of the icicle at the eave.

For a spring that starts on a snowy day.

For a spring eternal in the Word of Your beloved Child.

On this day, Your Son the Light of the World

was presented in the Temple:

let me rejoice in the coming of light!

On this day, sweet Brigid's eternal flames

bring new life to the Earth:

may I rejoice in the coming of light!

All praise and all thanksgiving to the God of the Springtime,

as the icicle drips at the eave and the dawn comes ever-earlier!

PRAYER FOR THE ROWAN MOON

A modern prayer.

Bright glory, bright moon,
Moon of Brigid,
lamp of the poor,
my love, my light,
illumined by God.
Bright moon of glory,
teach me good purpose
toward each creature in Creation.
Bright moon of grace,
teach me good prayer
in accord with Christ's heart.

Fiery moon of great light,
be in my heart.
be in my deeds,
be in my wishes.
Teach me your grace.
Bright moon of Brigid,
your light my hope,
your light on my purpose below,
in accord with God's satisfaction.

Bright fire, bright moon,
point my heart to God's repose.
Point me to my rest,
with the Son of Tranquility.

PRAYER FOR THE DAYS OF THE ROWAN MOON

A modern prayer.

This is the month for clarity,
for pure hearts,
for unclouded vision.
Wash my heart clean, O Great God.
Wash my heart, O Three-in-One,
that I may be pure as You are pure.
Clear all distortion from my vision;
may I see with the bright eyes of Brigid,
the bright eyes of Mary,
the brightest eyes of Christ.
Make clean all that is soiled;
give focus to all that has blurred;
make chaste all that has wandered astray.
This is the month for clarity,
for pure hearts,
for unclouded vision.

The Ash Moon

The ash is one of the three trees sacred to the Druids (ash, oak, and thorn), and according to Norse tradition, Yggdrasil, the world tree, was an ash. The ash, which is also known by the Celtic name Nion (pronounced "knee-un"), represents the connection between heaven and earth, for it has both towering branches and large roots that sink deep into the ground. It is a symbol of stability and security. Because of the heavenly energy flowing through it from its tall branches, it was considered to be useful as protection against evil. An Elizabethan herbalist, John Gerard, wrote that snakes were so afraid of the ash tree that they would not dare even to slither over its morning or evening shadow. Wearing ash leaves near the body—in a pocket or stuffed in a boot—was viewed as a deterrent against evil. Ash leaves were also worn in shoes to relieve sore or itchy feet. Because of the ash tree's strength and power, its month is a good time to connect with your own sources of strength, both in this world and the Otherworld.

The Spring Equinox and the Ash Moon

(MARCH)

At the Spring Equinox, the Sun, source of Earth's light and life, once more aligns directly with the tilt of the Earth's rotational orbit, giving us equal periods of light and dark. As the Sun crosses the celestial equator, day and night are balanced.

This is a joyful holy day that focuses on rebirth and growth. The Earth is alive again! It is a time to wake up and celebrate. The time of dark and rest is over, and now, we are called to new energy and purpose. Embrace new beginnings. See what is asking to be reborn in your life. Allow yourself to hope, to be curious, and to feel excited about new ideas. Bring into the light all that occupied you during the long dark months; in the clarity of spring's new light, evaluate how you can use your energy to bring dreams into reality. What seeds do you want to plant?

According to Pagan practice, this is also a time when our world's dualism comes into balance—masculine and feminine, dark and light, soft and hard, all are at rest and in harmony.

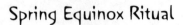

Spring Equinox Ritual

Plant seeds. Even if you don't have a garden, two or three flower or bean seeds can grow in a flowerpot. As you plant your seeds, meditate on what you want to "plant" in your own life. What do you want to germinate and grow? Now you need to tend your seeds faithfully, Each day, as you water and watch them grow, meditate on your own growth. Offer it up in prayer.

Some other Celtic celebrations fall during this month. March 1 is St. David's Day, honoring Wale's patron saint who died on this date in 589. His last words to his followers were, "Be joyful, keep the faith and do the little things that you have heard and seen me do." Wearing a daffodil is a traditional way to honor David.

And then of course, there's March 17, St. Patrick's Day. Around the globe, it's not only the Irish who celebrate on this day; much of the world joins in. Whether you attend a parade, eat Irish foods, or simply wear green, March 17 is a day to honor Patrick, the fifth-century man who helped bring Christianity to Ireland. It's also a time to experience the sheer magic of greenness—what Hildegard of Bingen called "viriditas," the Divine freshness, vitality, fruitfulness, and growth that we see displayed everywhere at springtime.

Finally, March 20 is St. Cuthbert's Day. Cuthbert was a seventh-century Anglo-Saxon who was educated at the Celtic monastery of Melrose, and throughout his life, he sought to reconcile the Celts and the Anglos in the peace of Christ. His natural inclination was to live the solitary life of a hermit, but he was obedient to God's call and was consecrated bishop of Lindisfarne. His dying words on March 20 were: "Always preserve divine charity among yourselves, and when you come together to discuss your common affairs, let your principal goal be to reach a unanimous decision." In our modern polarized world, his feast day is a time to hear our own call to bridge-building and reconciliation.

PRAYER FOR THE ASH MOON

Based on an ancient prayer.

Hail, new moon of the new month,

guiding jewel of gentleness,

I am bending my knee,

I am offering my love.

I am giving you my hand.

I am lifting up my eyes to you,

O new moon of the ash.

You are traveling your course,

steering the tides,

queen-maiden of guidance,

queen-maiden of good fortune,

queen-maiden of good magic,

queen-maiden of love and God's grace.

ST. DAVID'S PRAYER

A modern prayer.

Giver of Life,
I ask that you help me
to be joyful
even in the midst of frustration,
even in discouragement,
even in sorrow.
Give me strength
to remain faithful to love,
steadfast in hope.
I ask you not for the ability
to do great things,
but only that I may
keep on doing little things,
one by one,
that demonstrate Your love.
Giver of Life,
this I ask you
that I may be joyful and faithful,
and continue doing the little things
You give to me to do.

ST. PATRICK'S PRAYER

An ancient prayer attributed to St. Patrick.

May the Strength of God pilot us.

May the Power of God preserve us.

May the Wisdom of God instruct us.

May the Hand of God protect us.

May the Way of God direct us.

May the Shield of God defend us.

May the Host of God guard us

against the snares of the evil ones,

against temptations of the world.

May Christ be with us!

May Christ be before us!

May Christ be in us!

Christ be over all!

May your Salvation,

always be ours,

this day, O Christ, and evermore.

THE BREASTPLATE OF ST. PATRICK

An ancient prayer attributed to St. Patrick.

I arise today

through a mighty strength,

the invocation of the Trinity,

through belief in the Threeness,

through confession of the Oneness

of the Creator of creation.

I arise today

through the strength of Christ's birth with His baptism,

through the strength of His crucifixion with His burial,

through the strength of His resurrection with His ascension.

I arise today

through the strength of the love of cherubim,

in the obedience of angels,

in the service of archangels,

in the hope of resurrection to meet with reward,

in the prayers of those who went before,

in the truth of prophets,

in the preaching of apostles.

I arise today, through

the strength of heaven,

the light of the sun,

the radiance of the moon,

the splendor of fire,

the speed of lightning,

the swiftness of wind,

the depth of the sea,

the stability of the earth,

the firmness of rock.

I arise today, through

God's strength to pilot me,

God's might to uphold me,

God's wisdom to guide me,

God's eye to look before me,

God's ear to hear me,

God's word to speak for me,

God's hand to guard me,

God's shield to protect me,

God's host to save me

from snares of devils,

from temptation of vices,

from everyone who shall wish me ill,

afar and near.

I summon today

all these powers between me and those evils,

against every cruel and merciless power

that may oppose my body and soul,

against every knowledge that corrupts body and soul;

Christ to shield me today

against poison, against burning,

against drowning, against wounding,

so that there may come to me an abundance of reward.

Christ with me,

Christ before me,

Christ behind me,

Christ in me,

Christ beneath me,

Christ above me,

Christ on my right,

Christ on my left,

Christ when I lie down,

Christ when I sit down,

Christ when I arise,

Christ in the heart of every man who thinks of me,

Christ in the mouth of everyone who speaks of me,

Christ in every eye that sees me,

Christ in every ear that hears me.

PRAYER TO ST. CUTHBERT

A modern prayer.

Faithful Cuthbert,
help us to resist
the temptation to argue.
Instead, teach us to build bridges.
Wash from our hearts
the scorn, the frustration,
and the contempt
that lead only to wider cracks
in our human community.
Give us strength and wisdom
to be more like you,
a warrior for reconciliation.

AWAKENING THE GROUND

Based on an ancient prayer.

Be whole, soft earth,
our mother.
Be a-growing in the lap of God.
Be filled with fodder
to meet our need.
Be full-fed, sweet earth,
and bring forth food and fodder.
Blossom bright;
blessed become;
and the God who wrought the ground,
grant us the gifts of growing,
that the corn and all plants
may come to meet our need.

PRAYER FOR THE SPRING EQUINOX

A modern prayer.

Thanks to You, O God, for the rising of new life,

for life itself, in limb and lungs,

in new grass and bright blossom,

in swelling bellies of sheep and cow.

May all joy be to Your glory, O God of every gift,

and to the glory of my soul likewise.

O great God, aid my soul

with the aiding of Your own mercy.

And as the sun scatters the mist on the crest of the hills,

may each ill haze clear from my soul, O God.

SPRING BLESSING

A modern prayer.

May we today, at the dawn of new life,
bless the Earth.
Teach us, O Creator God,
to enrich the soil,
to put back what we have taken.
We depend on Your hand for our sustenance.
We depend on Your Earth for our sustenance.

The seed is in the Earth's belly,
and You have planted new life in our hearts.
We give You thanks
and ask that You bless the Earth,
bless human hands that work the Earth,
and bless the life You give.

The Alder Moon

In springtime, the alder tree flourishes on riverbanks, often with its roots in the water. Its root system provides rich nutrients to the soil, and it is known for its ability to restore poor soil conditions. When its roots are submerged in wetlands, they create shelter systems for fish, while the leaves easily decompose in the water, adding nutrients that benefit water creatures. The alder's generosity serves as an example to human lives. Alder flowers and twigs were used for charms against faeries' mischief, and the wood was traditionally used for creating whistles and flutes. Because both female and male flowers grow on the same branch, the alder tree also symbolizes the balance between feminine and masculine energies. During the Alder Month, called **Fearn** *by the Celts (pronounced "fairin"), focus on balance, on generosity, and on the light of new life.*

Ostara (Easter) and the Alder Moon

(APRIL)

Easter falls on different dates. Technically, it can be as early as March 21—or as late as April 19. Its date is determined by the lunar cycle; it falls on the first Sunday after the full moon that falls on or after the Spring Equinox.

According to the sixth-century historian Bede the Venerable, Easter takes its name from *Eostre*, an ancient springtime goddess whose name was honored on ancient shrines across Europe. Her name means "to shine"; the word *east* comes from the same root.

Although Easter is a Christian holiday, it also has a Pagan name—Ostara—and many of the traditional Easter symbols, such as eggs and rabbits, have their roots in Pagan spirituality.

As both a Christian and Pagan holy day, this is a time of great fertility and new growth. It is a time for newborn animals—from chicks to lambs to bunnies—and it is a time of hope and light.

The Christian holiday celebrates the resurrection of Jesus—the miraculous triumph of life over death—and at this time of the year's turning wheel, the resurrection of new life is everywhere we turn, from road banks to farmers' fields.

Winter-brown lawns turn green; bare branches burst into bloom; birds return north and lay their eggs; and once-frozen ponds come alive with the chorus of frogs.

As John Carey writes in *A Single Ray of the Sun*:

> The revolutions of the heavenly bodies, the flowing and replenishment of streams, the recurring sequence of the seasons: surely the clue to these cosmic mysteries is . . . resurrection. . . . Resurrection, far from being an alien and uncanny prodigy, is an integral feature of the cyclical workings of nature: all things bear witness to it, did we but see. It is at the time of Christ's resurrection that warmth and light and flowers come again: the link between Easter and the vernal equinox has its basis in the universe's fundamental harmonies. . . . The [miracle of miracles], the return from death to life, is not imposed by arbitrary fiat, but found with the inmost fabric of creation.

Ostara-Easter Ritual

Find out the exact time for the sunrise, and then set your alarm for a half hour earlier. Sit in the darkness, somewhere outside where you can see the horizon or beside an east-facing window, and watch the slowly growing light creep up into the sky. As the blazing Sun lifts above the horizon line, stand up and greet it with open arms and a prayer for new life and light within your own heart.

Another Celtic holiday falls in April—St. Mangus Day on April 16. Mangus was an eleventh-century Viking who converted to Christ. He had a reputation for piety and gentleness, which the Norwegians viewed as cowardice. During a Viking raid on Wales, he refused to fight and instead, stayed on board the ship, praying and singing psalms. Afterward, he was obliged to take refuge in Scotland. Later, when confronted by his enemies, he again refused to take up the sword and was murdered on Orkney. He died praying for his killers. Magnus was first buried on the spot where he died on April 16. According to the *Carmina Gadelica*:

> The place where Magnus was slain had been a rough, sterile moor of heath and moss, but immediately Magnus was put to death the moor became a smiling grassy plain, and there issued a heavenly light and a sweet odour from the holy ground. Those who were in peril prayed to Magnus and were rescued, and those who were sick came to his grave and were healed. Pilgrims flocked to his tomb to keep vigil at his shrine, and be cured of their leprosy of body or of soul.

Eventually, Magnus's bones ended up in the cathedral at Kirkwall. His life and death are still celebrated on Orkney.

PRAYER OF THE ALDER MOON

*Based on an ancient prayer from a time when many people
died over the hard winter months.*

When I see the spring moon,
I do well to lift my eyes;
I do well to bend my knee;
I do well to bow my head;
I do well to give God praise,
that I have lived to see the spring moon,
lovely leader of the new season.

Many a man and woman have gone forth
over the black river of the abyss
since last you shone on me,
spring moon of the alder.
Many have gone beyond this life,
since the spring moon last shone,
but I am still enjoying Earth.
I am still glad to see the spring moon,
moon of bright blessing.

PRAYER IN SPRINGTIME FLOODS

Adapted from the Carmina Gadelica.

In springtime comes the great storms.
On Monday, when the airy firmament pours rain,
we shall be obedient to Christ the King,
listening to Your voice, O God,
in wind and rain and flood.

On Tuesday will come the hail,
heart-paining, skin-piercing,
wringing blood from the flocks,
and still, O God, we listen to Your voice.

On Wednesday will blow the wind,
sweeping all things bare,
showering gusts of gall and grief,
thunder that bursts and rends the hills,
and still, O God, we listen to Your voice.

On Thursday pours more rain,
driving people and creatures into flight,
like early leaves stripped off the trees,
and still, O God, we listen to Your voice.

On Friday will come the cloud of darkness;
dread will come over the world;
floods will loosen stones to tumble over field and farm.
This is the day of Your death, sweet Jesu,
but still we listen to Your voice.

On Saturday, the flood will rise
like a great sea,
rushing like a mighty river
where no river flowed before.
Let us be at our best, O God,
as we hasten to Your hill of safety,
and may we listen for Your voice.

On Sunday, will arise the Son of light and glory,
with warm air and sweet promise
that floods will fall and life return, O God,
as we listen to Your voice.

PRAYER FOR EASTER SUNDAY

A modern prayer.

Pray I this day my prayer to You, O God.
I give voice this day as though I spoke with Your voice.
Keep I this day as the people of heaven keep it.
Spend I this day as Your own household spends it.
Go I this day according to Your love, O God.
Pass I this day as pass the saints in heaven.
Loving Christ, Who died on Friday upon the tree,
each day and each night I remember Your covenant to me.
In my lying down and rising up I yield myself to Your cross.
In my life and my death, in my health and my ill,
You are my peace.
May I remember this day, and each day,
that You are the source of all mercies.

The warmth of sun, the bud, the seed,
all things swelling, the cow with calf,
the sheep with lamb, my heart with love,
all this You bestowed gently and generously.
This day and each day may I be fuller in love with You.
Each thing I have received, from You it came,
each thing for which I hope, from Your love it will come.

Each thing I enjoy is from Your bounty.
Each thing I ask comes in Your time.
Holy God, loving One, Word Everlasting,
grant me to have from You this living prayer:
lighten my understanding, kindle my will,
begin my doing, incite my love,
strengthen my weakness, enfold my desire,
on this day and every day.

PRAYER FOR EASTERTIDE

Adapted from an ancient prayer.

Early on the morn of Easter Monday,
I saw on the salt water
a duck and a white swan
swimming together.
Remember to love the unlike and the like.

I heard on Easter Tuesday
the warbler, the swallow, and the swift,
trilling on high and calling.
Remember to listen for the voice of God.

On Easter Wednesday, day of glory,
I walked along the strand
and saw three terns arise from among the waves.
Remember to see the Three of Glory.

On Bright Thursday, day of joy,
I saw the marsh violet blooming
and the cherry tree.
Remember to praise the Lord of New Life.

On Bright Friday, day of Mary,
I drank clean water
from the forest spring.
Remember Mary, the Life-Giving Spring.

On Bright Saturday, day of feasting,
I ate my fill
of meat and bread and milk.
Remember the Bread of Life
come down to us from Heaven.

The circling of Bridget calm,
the circling of Mary mild,
the circling of Michael strong,
be round me and mine,
round me and mine at Eastertide.

PRAYER TO OSTARA I

A modern prayer.

Lady of Light,
give us strength
and new energy.
Lead us into spring's warmth and light,
as we leave winter-dark behind.
Release us from all that weighs us down.
Free us, we pray, from all that hinders,
all that cramps and locks and limits.
Lead us to the dawn.

PRAYER TO OSTARA II

A modern prayer.

Bright Lady, Warm Lady,
Fertile One, Springtime's Love,
bring to us all that births,
that shines, that blooms.
We seek your precious eggs,
your dancing hares;
we listen for your song on the wind.
Winter has done his work
and now he sleeps
till his time comes once again.
Bring fruit now to our winter labor.
Bring blossom to our hearts.
Bring us to new life.
Let us be your messengers,
your midwifes,
birthing new life into a wintry world.

PRAYER TO ST. MAGNUS

From the Carmina Gadelica.

O Magnus of my love,
you are the one who would guide us,
you fragrant body of grace,
remember us.
Remember us, thou saint of power,
who did encompass and protect the people,
succour us in our distress,
nor forsake us.

Lift our flocks to the hills,
quell the wolf and the fox,
ward off the specter, the giant, fury,
and oppression.
Surround cows and herds,
surround sheep and lambs;
keep from them all danger.

Sprinkle dew from the sky upon our cattle.
Give growth to grass and corn, and sap to plants,
to watercress, deergrass, reeds, burdock, and daisy.
O Magnus of fame,
from the ship of the heroes,
on the crests of the waves,
on the sea, on the land,
aid and preserve us.

The Willow Moon and the Hawthorn Moon

Two Celtic moons usually fall during May, the Willow at the beginning (overlapping with the end of April) and the Hawthorn toward the end, overlapping with the first week of June. The Willow Moon was known to the Celts as **Saille** *(pronounced "sahl-yeh"), and the Hawthorne Moon was* **Huath** *(pronounced "Hoh-uh").*

The Willow Moon is associated with rain and wetness, as well as the healing of pain. Willow bark contains salicin, which is a chemical similar to aspirin (acetylsalicylic acid). In combination with the herb's powerful anti-inflammatory plant compounds (called flavonoids), salicin is thought to be responsible for the willow's pain-relieving and anti-inflammatory effects. Because new trees can grow from broken branches, the willow is associated with immortality. The tree is also known for its flexibility. As Ralph Waldo Emerson wrote, "I am a willow of the wilderness, Loving the wind that bent me."

Meanwhile, the Hawthorn Moon governs a time of magic and masculine energy. The hawthorn is one of the three trees associated with the Otherworld. (The others are ash and oak.) Sometimes called a "clootie tree," traditionally, scraps of fabric were hung from lone hawthorn trees, symbolic of prayers offered. It is a prickly sort of tree that blooms in May with white blossoms, and a common tree in English hedges; its name traces back to the Old English word **hagathorn***, a combination of* **haga** *("hedge") and* **thorn***. The flowers, leaves and fruits of the hawthorn have properties that reduce blood pressure and stimulate the heart, as well as act as a mild sedative. (But do not try to self-medicate!) The berries (also known as "Pixie Pears") contain vitamin B complex and vitamin C. Hawthorn is sacred to the Welsh sun goddess Olwen, the "white lady of the day"; according to legend, where she trod she left white footprints of hawthorn blossom. Hawthorn branches are also traditionally said to have been used for Jesus' crown of thorns.*

Beltane, the Willow Moon, and the Hawthorn Moon

(MAY)

Beltane is a celebration that falls midway between the Spring Equinox and the Summer Solstice. It is a time to honor the peak of springtime and the coming summer, a day to celebrate the new life that is emerging and the fertility that lies ahead. Festivities may begin on the last night of April and continue through May 1.

The Celtic word *Beltane* means "fires of Bel" (Bel was a Celtic deity.) Traditionally, it has been a fire festival, a time for the God and the Goddess to wed, with a promise of future fruitfulness. It was also a time for lovers' courting, and the festivities often led to marriages. Cattle were sometimes passed between two fires, because the fire and smoke were thought to ensure the herd's fertility.

Across Celtic lands, modern celebrations of Beltane often include dancing around a May pole, as well as the ritual of a "marriage" between the May Queen and the May King (also known as Jack in the Green), symbolizing the promise of the land's summer fruitfulness. On this ancient holy day, modern Pagans celebrate Beltane with bonfires, dance, and ritual.

People may leap over the fires to bring fertility to body, mind, and spirit.

Beltane is also known as May Day, and Christians have celebrated Mary on this day, crowning her with flowers (much as the May Queen is crowned). It is perhaps no accident that Mother's Day falls during the month of May, for this is a time to celebrate the Divine Mother, giver of life and fruitfulness.

May Day Ritual

Fill baskets with flowers, and adorn your home with them. An old custom is to gift a May basket secretly: place the basket on the front door on May Day morning, ring the door bell, and then disappear before the door is answered. Let the flowers be a reminder to honor the Divine Feminine, as well as courageous women like Dymphna who have suffered injustice.

Another Celtic holy day that falls during the month of May is the feast day of St. Dymphna. According to tradition, Dymphna was the daughter of a seventh-century Irish king named Damon. When Dymphna was fifteen, her mother died—and her father proposed that she marry him in her mother's stead. Dymphna fled to Belgium, but her father followed her there. On May 15, when Dymphna persisted in her refusal of her father's proposition,

Damon drew his sword and struck off her head. (The beheading of a woman was often a medieval euphemism for rape.) Shortly after her death, five "lunatics" wandered into the countryside where she was killed and slept the night there, only to awaken cured. A church was built on this site; it burned in 1489, but was rebuilt in 1532. It is still there, and has been joined by a house for the mentally ill. Today, Dymphna is known as the patron saint of victims of incest, teen runaways, and those suffering from psychological problems. Her feast day is a reminder to work for justice and compassion for those in our world who are vulnerable, who have experienced sexual assault and emotional affliction.

May is also the month of St. Brendan's Day, on the sixteenth. Brendan is believed to have been born in the year 484, in Ireland. He became one of the Twelve Apostles of Ireland, Christian elders who absorbed into themselves the Druids' role as wisdom-keepers. Brendan's vocation called him not only to a life of prayer but also to a life of constant journeying. A skilled navigator, he first sailed around Ireland's scattered islands, building monasteries wherever he could. Next, he sailed still further, to the Arran Islands, Wales, and Brittany. In each place he went, he built communities of faith and learning. Late in his life, the story goes, Brendan heard tales of a marvelous land to the west, a land that was the original Garden of Eden and also the Paradise to which he believed all life lead. After spending time in prayer, Brendan felt called to build a currach (a round-bottomed boat with square sails, waterproofed with skins). With a crew of Christian brothers, he set sail for the Promised Land, the Isle of the Blessed. Today, some historians believe that Brendan did in fact reach the Americas. They give credence to the saint's voyage based on Viking sagas that tell of finding Christian communities in Iceland, communities founded by the Irish before the Vikings' arrival. The greatest argument against the historicity of Brendan's great voyage, however, was the nature of his boat. Experts were skeptical that such a primitive craft would have been able to cross the Atlantic. In 1976, however, Tim Severin built a replica of a fifth-century Irish currach, set sail from Ireland, made stops at Iceland and Greenland, and eventually, a year after he began his voyage, reached Newfoundland—using only fifth-century technology. Brendan's story is a form of *immram*, a sea journey to a hidden world. The Christian Celts' immram stories carried on a still more ancient pagan legacy of mysterious journeys to the Otherworld. These stories are all a form of what Joseph Campbell called the "hero's journey"—and according to Campbell, we each have our own journey to make. Like Brendan, we are all called to venture out past our familiar boundaries, into new territories where we discover amazing treasures, learn new things, and return changed.

WILLOW MOON BLESSING

A modern prayer.

Look up and see the Willow Moon,
the King of life blessing her;
fragrant be every night
upon which she shines!
May her luster be full
to each one in need;
may her course complete,
around all beset with trouble.
May her light above
shine on everyone in dire danger;
may her bright guidance
illumine all need.
May the Willow Moon
shine through the rain clouds,
on me and on every one
clouded with dark tears.
May her light be God's hand
in every danger I face,
now and in the hour of my death,
and on the day of my resurrection.

BELTANE BLESSING I

Adapted from the Carmina Gadelica.

Bless, O Threefold true and bountiful,

myself, my spouse, and my children,

all those I hold dear,

on the fragrant plain, on the joyful lonely places,

on the fragrant plain, on the joyful lonely places.

Everything within my dwelling, everything I own,

all crops and flocks,

Three Persons, take into Your possession now

all that to me belongs,

from Beltane until Hallow's Eve.

Be the sure Trinity protecting me in truth.

Satisfy my soul with Your Word.

I ask Your gentle blessing,

from sea to river mouth,

from wave to waterfall.

Shield my loved ones beneath the wing of Your glory.

Bless everything and everyone who crosses my lintel.

Place the cross of Christ on us with the power of love,

until we see the land of joy.

If we should lose cow or sheep or goat,

in attack from storm or creatures wild,

may the tending of the Triune follow them.

You are the Being who created me at the beginning.

Hear me each May morning.

Let each fresh morning rise in me;

each gentle dusk fall in me;

in Your own presence, O God of life,

in Your own presence, O God of life.

BELTANE BLESSING II

Adapted from the Carmina Gadelica.

Mary, mother of saints, mother of each of us,
Bless our flocks and cattle;
bless all we say we own.
Let not hate come near us.
Drive from our hearts all cruelty.
Keep your eye on us this May,
Every Monday and Tuesday,
go with us wherever we go;
every Wednesday and Thursday,
put your gracious hand always all around
each cow and calf, each sheep and lamb.
Tend all we call our own.

Each Friday, lead our sheep;
be at their head, while their lambs follow after;
encompass them with God's encompassing.
every Saturday be with them too.
Bring the goats with their young to grassy seaside
and green hill summits.
The strength of the Triune be our shield in all distress.
The strength of Christ, His peace, and His resurrection;
the strength of the Spirit, Physician of all health;
and the strength of the Creator, High Ruler of grace;

and the blessing of Patrick,
the blessing of Brigid,
the blessing of Brendan,
the blessing of Columba,
the blessing of all saints be with us through the summer days,
and all the summer nights.

Bless ourselves and our children.
Bless the man whose name we bear.
Bless the woman from whose womb we came.
Give us every holiness, blessing, and power,
in the summer days ahead, in every time and hour,
in the name of the Holy Threefold,
Creator, Christ, and Spirit everlasting.
May the Cross of Christ shield us in each downward moment.
May the Cross of Christ shield us in each upward moment.
May the Cross of Christ shield us in each sideway moment.
May the Cross of Christ shield us when we are at a standstill.
Bless us, we pray,
and accept from us in return,
our Beltane blessing.

BELTANE BLESSING III

A modern prayer.

Bless, O Divine One, Queen of All,
on this day of fire and flower,
my family and myself
my pets, my plants,
all wild things that share my world,
and all children of the Great Mother.
Bless everything within my dwelling,
all my possessions, all my work.
I give them now to You,
a crown of flame and flower.
I ask that you shield my loved ones
between the Beltane fires.
On this May Day,
bless everything and every one I touch.
May your tending follow them.
May your blessing make them fruitful.
May your love embrace them.
You who gave me birth
give birth now, I pray,
to Your work of fire and flower
in each detail of my life.
Bless, O Divine One, Queen of Love,
on this day of fire and flower.

BELTANE BLESSING IV

From the Carmina Gadelica.

Valiant Michael of the white steeds,
who subdued the Dragon of blood,
for love of God, for pains of Mary's Son,
spread thy wing over us, shield us all,
spread thy wing over us, shield us all.
Mary beloved! Mother of the White Lamb,
shield, oh shield us, pure Virgin of nobleness,
and Brigid the beauteous, shepherdess of the flocks.
Safeguard our cattle, surround us together,
safeguard our cattle, surround us together.
And Columba, beneficent, benign,
in the name of Creator, Christ, and of Spirit Holy,
through the Three-in-One, through the Trinity,
encompass ourselves, shield our procession,
encompass thou ourselves, shield our procession
from winter into summer.
Creator! O Christ! O Spirit Holy!
Be the Triune with us day and night,
on the lowlands or on the mountain ridge
be the Triune with us and God's arm around our head,
be the Triune with us and God's arm around our head.

Creator! O Christ! O Spirit Holy!
Be with us, Three-One, day and night,
and on the back of the wave as on the mountain side.
Our Mother shall be with us with her arm under our head,
and on the back of the wave as on the mountain side
our Mother shall be with us with her arm under our head.

MAYTIME PRAYER

From an ancient Welsh prayer.

Maytime is a fair season,
with its bird song and bright trees,
with the plow in the furrow,
while the sea is green
and many colors clothe the Earth.
The gift I ask of this Maytime,
may it not be denied me,
is peace between myself and God,
between myself and all I meet,
between myself and the sweet Earth.
May this Maytime show me the way
to the gate of glory
that leads to Your court, O Christ.

MAY SONG

From an ancient Welsh song.

May-Day, delight! Beautiful color!
The blackbirds sing. The cuckoos sing.
The brilliance of the season ever welcome!
On the edge of the branching woods
the swallows skim the air;
the heather spreads her long hair;
the planets in their courses running,
they shape us here;
the sea is lulled to rest,
and flowers cover the Earth.

THE CONSECRATION OF THE SEED

Adapted from the Carmina Gadelica.

I will go out to sow the seed,
In the name of the One who gives it growth.
I will face into the wind,
and throw a gracious handful on high,
in trust that God will make it fall
on fertile earth,
where dew and rain will make it swell.
The dew will come down to welcome,
each seed that lies in sleep.
every seed will take root in the earth,
as the Ruler of the elements desires.
Green sprouts will come forth with the dew.
They will inhale life from the soft wind.
By God's grace the Earth produces:
first the stalk, then the ear,
then the full grain shall appear.

I will come round the fields, rightways with the sun,

in the name of Ariel and the angels nine,

in the name of Gabriel and the Apostle king.

Creator, Christ, and Spirit Holy,

give growth and kind sustenance

to everything that grows in my ground

until the day of gladness shall come,

the feast day of Michael, day of harvest.

THE BLESSING OF THE PLOUGH

Adapted from the Carmina Gadelica.

Blessed be, God of all creation.

Give softness to the land.

Give us skill to work the land.

This plough is sign to us of Your blessing.

Give us softness of heart.

Give us skill to serve You.

Blessed be God—Creator, Christ, and Holy Spirit,

Three of Glory, Three of Light, Three of Life.

Blessed be the Bright Three forever.

God speed the plough.

God speed the plough.

PRAYER TO ST. DYMPHNA (MAY 15)

A modern prayer.

Dear One, young saint,
courageous one,
you knew the pain of injustice,
the violence of violation,
the loss of respect for boundaries,
and yet you remained true to yourself.
We ask your blessing now
on all those who, like you,
are in danger of violation;
protect them and bring them justice.
We ask your blessing now
on all those who, like you,
have been violated.
Restore them, we pray,
and heal their hearts and flesh.
May they, like you,
find that they still have
healing work to do,
that their wounds
can make them strong enough
to give to others who suffer too.

Dear One, young saint,
may they, like you,
be blessed with courage,
with determination,
and with healing love.

PRAYER OF ST. BRENDAN

Ancient prayer accredited to St. Brendan.

Help me to journey beyond the familiar
and into the unknown.
Give me the faith to leave old ways
and break fresh ground with You.
Christ of the Mysteries, I trust You
to be stronger than each storm within me.
I will trust in the darkness
and know that my times,
even now, are in Your hand.
Tune my spirit to the music of heaven,
and somehow, make my obedience
count for You.

PRAYER OF THE HAWTHORNE MOON

A modern prayer.

She that I love is the new moon,
the King of all creatures blessing her;
may I do good
to each creature in Creation.
Holy be each thing
that she illumines;
kind be each deed
that she reveals.
May she come through thick clouds
to me and to every mortal
who wanders in dark affliction.
May she come through dark clouds
to me and to each one
who stumbles in tribulation.
May she show me the way
to the Queen of grace.

The Oak Moon

The Oak Moon is the time when the trees reach their full blooming stage, a time of warmth and life. The mighty oak is one of the most powerful trees, typically towering over all its neighbors. The Celtic word for this month was **Duir**, *the root word of Druid (who were "oak knowers"), as well as our words for "endure" and "truth"; thus, the oak is connected with both strength and enduring truth. This is a month to build strong roots, while at the same time reaching ever upward.*

The Summer Solstice and the Oak Moon

(JUNE)

In the Northern Hemisphere, the Summer Solstice occurs when the Earth's axis tilts the Northern Hemisphere closest to the sun, making this the longest day of the year, the turning point when the sun shines longest. The word *solstice* comes from the Latin words *sol*, meaning "sun," and *stitium* or *sistere*, meaning "still" or "stopped." After this day, the sun switches from a southward to northward trajectory in the sky. This was a marker to ancient people; the sky was their calendar, letting them know how to live in harmony with the Earth's cycle.

The Summer Solstice was a time of celebration. It was also a time when magic broke through from the Otherworld, and faeries might be glimpsed dancing in the moonlight. The Celts built bonfires on hilltops and at crossroads, believing the flames opened pathways toward the Light that shines at the heart of all life. To leap over the fire was a way to purify one's soul, burning away flaws and difficulties. Sometimes couples launched themselves over the fire with hands clasped as a way to bring their union good luck and enduring love.

The Celts believed that many medicinal plants were most effective if they were collected during the Summer Solstice. Many of these plants, including St. John's wort, verbena, and rue, are still valued today for their medicinal qualities.

Summer Solstice Ritual

This is a time to celebrate Divine Light. You can do so by building a bonfire and gathering around it with friends and family. A drum circle adds to the sense of joyful meaning. Or you might celebrate more privately by making a personal altar decorated with candles and wild flowers. Spend time in front of your altar meditating on the areas of growth in your life and the channels that you want to open to Divine Fire.

Columba's Feast Day is another celebration that falls during the month of June. St. Columba was a sixth-century Irish abbot who is credited with spreading Christianity throughout what is today Scotland. He founded the important abbey at Iona, which became an intellectual, artistic, and spiritual center for centuries. The Book of Kells and the Book of Durrow, both great masterpieces of Celtic art, are associated with Columba. Although Columba died many centuries ago, for many Celts he continued to be a living and beloved presence in their lives. Today, June 9, the anniversary of his death, has been designated as International Celtic Art Day.

Another Christian feast day is celebrated shortly after the Summer Solstice, on June 24—the Feast Day of John the Baptist. Traditionally, this is considered to be the birthdate of the man who was the forerunner of Jesus. He called for people to change their course, to turn in another direction and follow the Son of Light, so it is appropriate for his feast day to fall at the time that the sun changes direction in the sky.

PRAYER FOR THE DAY OF COLUMBA (JUNE 9)

From the Carmina Gadelica.

Columba kind and good,

send our sheep into the fields with health;

send a healthy calf to each cow;

make strong the threads upon our looms;

go with us as we launch our coracles into the salty sea.

This is the day to bear all things with patience.

This is the day to climb the heights.

This is the day to send our herds into the pasture.

This is the day to pray.

This is the day to die,

and this is the day to live.

This is your day, beloved Columba,

the day of our beloved.

MIDSUMMER INVOCATION

Adapted from the Carmina Gadelica.

Today is the day of grace,
the form of Christ before you,
the form of God behind you,
the stream of the Spirit through you,
to strengthen and aid you.
Grace upward over you,
grace downward over you,
grace of graces that cannot be dammed.
Grace of Creator,
grace of Son and Spirit,
grace of John of the Wilderness,
grace of sun,
grace of light,
grace of form and fortune,
grace of voice and word,
grace of Jesus Christ be always yours,
grace of the image of God be yours.

The excellence of John of the Wilderness,
the excellence of men,
the excellence of women,
the excellence of the lover,
the excellence of children,
the excellence of the sun in the sky,
be always yours.

Excellence of food,
excellence of drink,
excellence of music,
excellence of direction,
excellence of sea and land,
plain and hill, pasture and forest,
be yours today.

Excellence of sitting,
excellence of journeying,
excellence of cattle,
excellence of cooking,
excellence of curds and butter,
be yours today.

Excellence of travel,
excellence of home,
excellence of the small town,
excellence of the city,
excellence of sea and shore,
be ever yours.
Excellence of the duck of Mary,
excellence of the lamb of John,
excellence of sheep and wool,
excellence of the long days of light,
be always yours.

Grace of the summer skies be yours,
grace of the summer stars be yours,
grace of the summer moon be yours,
grace of the summer sun be yours,
grace of love and the crown of heaven be yours.

The bloom of God is upon you,
the bloom of Christ is upon you,
the bloom of the Spirit is upon you,
to bathe you and make you fair.

Christ is the summer star,
Christ is the brightness of each morn,
Christ is the news from every guest,
Christ is the question of every heart.

When you travel rough roads,
your feet will not be sore,
for Jesus is guarding you,
Jesus is close at hand.
The crown of God is around your head,
the diadem of the Son is around your brow,
the might of the Spirit is in your heart.
You shall go out and come home safe.
you are guarded from head-top to sole.
No hate nor jealousy nor envy
shall sunder your heart.
They shall not subdue you,
they shall not wound you.
No smith or craftsman shall make
any gear or tool,
weapon or device,
instrument or invention,
of copper or stone, brass or iron,
wood or bronze, gold or silver

that shall block you or enclose you,
that shall rend you or bridle you,
not down nor up,
above nor below,
in the sky aloft or the deep beneath.

You are the nut of Christ's heart,
the face of the sun,
the harp of God's music,
the crown of the Spirit's senses.
You are the love of the God of Life,
the love of the tender Christ,
the love of the Spirit Holy.
You are the love of John of the Wilderness,
the love of the summer sun.
You are the love of each living creature,
the love of each living creature.

PRAYER OF THE OAK MOON

A modern prayer.

May your light be fair to me!
May your course be smooth to me!
If your beginning is good,
seven times better be your end,
fair moon of the summer oak,
great lamp of grace!
The One who created you
created me likewise.
The One who gave you weight and light,
gave me life and death,
and the joy of all satisfaction,
great lamp of grace,
fair moon of the summer oak

The Holly Moon

Called **Tinne** *(pronounced "chihnn-uh")* by the Celts, the Holly Moon is a time to remember the immortality we see portrayed in Nature. An evergreen tree, the holly is as green in December as it is in July. The thorny leaves and red berries represent suffering. Christian symbolism connected the prickly leaves with Jesus' crown of thorns and the berries with the drops of blood he shed. In Celtic mythology, the Holly King was said to rule over the half of the year from the summer to the winter solstice, at which time the Oak King defeated the Holly King to rule for the time until the Summer Solstice again. It was forbidden to cut down a holly tree, but the branches were often brought inside to ensure peaceful relationships with the citizens of the Otherworld.

The Holly Moon

(JULY)

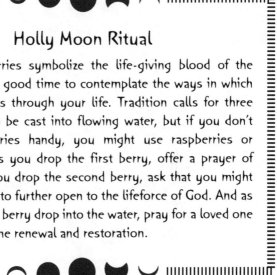

Holly Moon Ritual

Since holly berries symbolize the life-giving blood of the Divine, this is a good time to contemplate the ways in which Divine life flows through your life. Tradition calls for three holly berries to be cast into flowing water, but if you don't have holly berries handy, you might use raspberries or strawberries. As you drop the first berry, offer a prayer of gratitude. As you drop the second berry, ask that you might be shown ways to further open to the lifeforce of God. And as you let the final berry drop into the water, pray for a loved one who needs Divine renewal and restoration.

PRAYER TO THE HOLLY MOON

A modern prayer.

Bright Lady of the long night,
I give you praise for your light.
Bright Lady of the warm nights,
you lead me to the heights,
to places of refuge and rest.
By your light I am blessed.
By your life I am renewed.
Your blood my food,
your grace my delight,
Bright Lady of the long night.

SUMMER SONG I

Ancient Welsh prayer.

The birds sing good tidings,
the sea teams with life,
the wave-washed strands shines like silver,
the woods smile,
all evil flees,
apples swell,
corn fields flourish,
bees swarm, abundant and bright,
the world is cheerful,
and joyous peace fills every heart.

SUMMER SONG II

Ancient prayer attributed to the bard Taliesin.

Pleasant is the sun in the cloudless sky;

pleasant is the wheat on the stalk;

pleasant are seagulls at play;

pleasant is the moon shining on the world;

pleasant is the summer and the calm of long days;

pleasant are the fragrant bushes;

pleasant are the lonely doe and the stag;

pleasant is the vegetable garden where the leeks flourish;

pleasant are the young plants;

pleasant the heath and the sea marsh;

pleasant is the heart when it is filled with joy.

BIRD SONG

Ancient Welsh poem.

The summer thicket hides me,
the blackbird sings to me,
and I cannot contain my praise,
while the little birds trill their song.
The sweet gray bird's song
is as lovely a sermon as any priest's.
Truly its song directs my heart.
May my pen be like unto a gray bird's song.
May I write only praise of my Lord.

THE HERMIT'S SUMMER PLENTY

Ascribed to St. Manchin.

My little hut is hidden;
the tresses of a green-trunked yew uphold the sky;
safe am I here, with the green wall of an oak
against all storms.

A tree of apples gives me its bounty,
as rich as any mansion;
a pretty bush, branching and green,
bestows hazelnuts to me.
Water cresses sprout, bright yew berries,
and ivy as thick as a man's arm.
This is my little home, a place of summer plenty
and summer peace.

Around it lie wild swine and boars,
tamed and gentle,
with grazing deer, a badger's brood,
hares at play, field mice,
and all manner of small things:
a peaceful company, a calm assembly,
and bright foxes, delightful and quick,
a nimble gathering.

Pure water, salmon and trout;
a clutch of dove eggs, and handfuls of wild onions;
God has given them to me,
and apples, red whortleberries, crowberries,
strawberries, haws, sloes, nuts:
all these are my dainties.

Pleasant summer, dressed in a colored mantle
with sweet-tangled hair;
wild marjoram, fresh leeks:
good savory, green purity.

Songs of the bright red-breasted folk,
beloved wings,
the carol of the thrush like a friend's voice,
the swarm of bees, and the soft music of the world
is a gentle humming.

The wind in the pines
makes music for me.
All this is Christ's gift to me.
No strife is here, only summer calm.
No quarrels, no restless heart,
only my gratitude to Christ my Love
for all these summer gifts.

SUMMERTIME BLESSING

Adapted from the Carmina Gadelica.

Jesu, fragrant body of grace,
remember us in summer's sun.
Encompass us in storm;
protect us from wrath;
watch our flocks upon the hills;
let fox and wolf find food in forest wilds
but not our fields.
Guard us against all angry spirits,
against specters and giants,
against fairy arrows and darts,
and against oppression of any sort.

Encircle our cows and calves;
encircle our sheep and lambs;
encircle our children at their play.
Sprinkle dew from the sky each morning
to water the soil and the heart.
Give growth to grass and corn.
Give sap to trees.
Give green to burdock
and yellow to the daisy eye.
Let summer's sun remind us
of Jesu, fragrant body of grace.

The Hazel Moon

This month was known to the Celts as Coll, a time of wisdom and magic. It is the time of year when hazelnuts are ripening on the trees— and hazelnuts are associated with wisdom. In Celtic mythology, nine magical hazel trees hang over a sacred pool, dropping their hazelnuts into the water, where the magical nuts are eaten by the Salmon of Wisdom. Those who consume either the nuts or the fish will gain prophetic abilities. According to folklore, hazel trees could often be found with the apple and the hawthorn at the borders between worlds. The hazel is the tree found at the center of the Otherworld—or at World's End. Like willow, hazel is pliable, and is used for staffs, wands, baskets, and thatching. Forked twigs of hazel were also favored by diviners for finding water.

Lammas Day and the Hazel Moon

(AUGUST)

The first day of August is Lammas Day, an old Anglo-Saxons word that meant "loaf-mass." It was the medieval celebration of the wheat harvest, the first harvest festival of the year. Although this holy day was Christianized in the Middle Ages—and sometimes referred to as the "Feast of First Fruits"—its roots, like so many other festivals, are in Paganism. Its Celtic name was *Lughnasadh* (pronounced "loo-nass-ah"), which meant "assembly of Lugh." (Lugh was an Irish Sun God, a hero and a warrior.) This was a holy day of thanksgiving for the Earth's abundance.

The Lammas Loaf was the first loaf of bread made with the grain from the new harvest. Sometimes used for communion in the medieval church, it was believed to have magical properties. In a time when starvation was all too common, to know you had a secure source of food for the coming year must have been truly worthy of celebrating. After the formalities of presenting the loaves for blessing, the festivities would begin, with gift giving, processions, games, bonfires, and feasting. According to some traditions, villagers took the blessed bread and broke it into four pieces, with each of the pieces placed at the corner of a barn to protect the newly harvested grain. Lammas bread was often made in shapes, including wheat stalks, owls, and figures of the Corn God—or John Barleycorn.

The Sun God, Lugh, was known as John Barleycorn on Lammas Day. As the corn is cut, so John Barleycorn is cut down also. He is a Christ figure who surrenders his life so that others may be sustained by the grain, so that the life of the community can continue. He is both eaten as the bread and is then reborn as the seed returns to the earth.

Lammas Day is a reminder that everything dies in its season—and everything is reborn. It is the living enactment of Christ's words in the Gospel of John: "Most certainly I tell you, unless a grain of wheat falls into the earth and dies, it remains by itself alone. But if it dies, it bears much fruit."

In Scotland and northern parts of England, Lammas Day was often celebrated on August 15, where it came to be known as Marymas, a holy day that is still celebrated in many parts of Scotland. A special bread called "Marymas bannock" may be made, and there are displays of flowers, decorated wells, and candlelight processions. A girl is often crowned Queen of Marymas. Some people think the holiday was a celebration to honor Mary Queen of Scots, while for others, it is a feast day for Mary, Queen of Heaven. Traditionally, flower gardens and herbs are blessed on this day.

Lammas Day Ritual

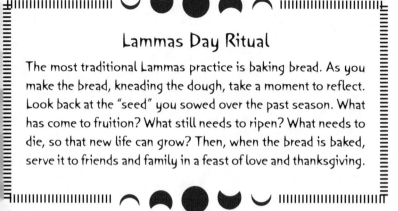

The most traditional Lammas practice is baking bread. As you make the bread, kneading the dough, take a moment to reflect. Look back at the "seed" you sowed over the past season. What has come to fruition? What still needs to ripen? What needs to die, so that new life can grow? Then, when the bread is baked, serve it to friends and family in a feast of love and thanksgiving.

The Feast Day of St. Aidan also falls during August, on the thirty-first. Aidan is credited with bringing Christianity to Scotland. Born in Ireland, he came to the Holy Island of Lindisfarne in 631 and built a monastery. According to the medieval historian Bede, Aidan carried his message to all people, "whether rich or poor, unbelievers or Christians," stirring "them up, by words and actions, to alms and good works. He was accustomed not only to teach the people committed to his charge in church, but also . . . to wander round the provinces, . . . and to sow the seeds of God's Word in their hearts, according to the capacity of each." On August 31 in 651, Aidan of Lindisfarne died, but his legacy continued to live on. His monastery on Lindisfarne was a spiritual and intellectual light for many generations.

PRAYER FOR THE HAZEL MOON

A modern prayer.

Moon of the last summer nights,
shield and sustain me this night.
God of power, shield and sustain me,
this night and every night.

Moon of the last summer nights,
make me holy with Your light.
God of light, heal my soul and my body,
each dark and each light.

Light before me, light behind,
God above me, God below,
shine on the path of God,
light upon my track.

LAMMAS BLESSING

Adapted from the Carmina Gadelic.

O God of the fast horse,
O God of the elements,
O God of the stars,
O God of the summer sun,
O Creator God!

Your joy my joy,
Your light my light,
Your peace my peace.
Your pain my pain,
Your love my love,
that last forever,
to the end of all endings,
the end of all endings.

You pour out Your grace in the light,
without stop or stint.
Your pour out Your grace in the fast horse,
speed without stop and without stint.

You are the Son of Light,
the Son of Life,
the Son of Death,
the Son of Grace,
who was and shall be,
with summer flow and autumn ebb,
with flow and with ebb,
with ebb and with flow,
forever and always.

LAMMAS DAY RESURRECTION

Traditional Pagan chant.

Hoof and horn,
hoof and horn,
all that dies shall be reborn.
Corn and grain, corn and grain,
all that falls shall rise again

LAMMAS DAY PRAYER

Adapted from the Carmina Gadelica.

High King,
O Bright One with the Strong Hand,
You are at our door.
Come in!
Shining One, World Wright,
Harper and Hero,
Star Smith, Lord of the Grain,
You are at our door.
Come in!

Lord of the Grain,
You surrender to the sickle.
You surrender to the earth.
You surrender to death.
Lord of Life, Shining One, High King,
take your queen,
Queen of the Grain, Lady of the Summer.

The land is full and must be tended;
The fields are gold and must be reaped.
Mother of the Field, Giver of Bread,
we thank you!

PICKING TOMATOES AT LAMMAS-TIDE

Modern prayer by William Palmer.

In the heat and haze of early August,

Lord, I praise Your Holy Name,

For this first harvest of tomatoes from my garden.

For the warm, brown earth they have grown from:

I give thanks to the Creator.

For the thundery summer rain that watered them:

I give thanks to the Child.

For the hot summer sun that has ripened the fruit:

I give thanks to the Spirit.

Each deep red globe,

gently twisted from under scented leaves,

a small miracle to hold in my own hand.

By Your bounteous grace, O Lord, and the sweat of my brow,

I have partnered with You in this miracle.

All praise to You, God of the green and growing Earth!

All praise to You, God of rain and sun and fruitfulness!

All praise to You, God of my backyard tomato harvest!

BLESSING FOR MARYMAS (AUGUST 15)

From the Carmina Gadelica.

On the feast day of Mary the fragrant,
Mother of the Shepherd of the flocks,
I cut a handful of the new corn,
I dried it gently in the sun,
I rubbed it sharply from the husk
between my palms.
I ground it in a mill on Friday,
I baked it on a piece of sheep-skin,
I toasted it over a fire of rowan,
and I shared it among my people.

I walked with the sun around my house,
in the name of Mary the Mother,
who promised to preserve me,
who did preserve me,
and who will preserve me,
in peace, in flocks,
in righteousness of heart,
in labor, in love,
in wisdom, in mercy,
for the sake of Your Passion.

O Christ of grace
who till the day of my death
will never forsake me!
Oh, till the day of my death
will never forsake me!

PRAYER TO THE SUMMER SUN

Adapted from the Carmina Gadelica.

The eye of the great God,
the eye of the God of glory,
the eye of the Creator of hosts,
the eye of the God of the living,
pouring upon us,
pouring upon us
gently and generously,
glory to you,
O glorious sun!
Glory to you,
the face of the God of life!

PRAYER TO LUGH

A modern Pagan prayer.

Great Lugh!
Master of artisans,
leader of craftsmen,
patron of smiths,
I call upon you and honor you this day.
You of the many skills and talents,
I ask you to shine upon me and
bless me with your gifts.
Give me strength in skill,
make my hands and mind deft,
shine light upon my talents.
O mighty Lugh,
I thank you for your blessings.

PRAYER FOR A SUMMER DAY

Adapted from the Carmina Gadelica.

On this summer morn,
bless to me, O God,
each thing my eyes see;
each fair tree and blooming flower;
each fragrant field and blue hill crest.

Bless to me, O God,
each sound my ears hear;
each murmuring dove, each lowing cow,
each laughing child.

Bless to me, O God,
each odor that goes in my nostrils,
the scent of green things growing.

Bless to me, O God,
each taste that goes into my lips,
the sweetness of milk and honey.

Bless to me each note that makes my song;
each ray of light that guides my way,
bless to me each thing that I pursue,
each lure that tempts my will;
the zeal that burns within my living soul.

Bless to me the Three who seek my heart,
the zeal that burns within my living soul,
the Three who seek my heart.

The Vine Moon

*This is a time of harvest, from grapes to apples and other tree fruit to vegetables. The Celts called this month **Muin** (pronounced "mwin"). The grapevine is a symbol of fertility and abundance, of interconnection and prosperity. The Vine Month is also a time of balance and equilibrium, as there are equal hours of darkness and light.*

The Autumn Equinox and the Vine Moon

(SEPTEMBER)

September is another point of perfect balance on the turning Wheel of the Year. As with the Spring Equinox in March, night and day are again equal in length, and we can experience the balance of all dualism—male and female, dark and light, inner and outer, everything in balance.

But equilibrium is always fleeting. The Autumn Equinox marks the turning point from summer to autumn. From now on, light will wane, and the nights will grow longer and cooler as the wheel turns toward the Winter Solstice again. We especially see the changes in the trees, as their leaves begin to turn from green to the colors of fire. The sap in their veins is slowing now, preparing for their long winter sleep.

The Celtic name for the Autumn Equinox is *Mabon*, the second harvest, a time of thanksgiving. Mabon was a Welsh god, the child of Light and the Earth. The word *Mabon* was not used for the Autumn Equinox until the 1970s, however, when it was adopted by modern Paganism.

The apple is sometimes considered to be the symbol of Mabon. This fruit figures in many sacred traditions as a symbol for life and immortality. According to Paganism, the apple also contains a secret meaning: if you cut it width-ways, you'll see that a star-shape, a pentagram, contains the seeds. The five points remind us of the five elements—air, earth, fire, and water, with the Spirit as the fifth point at the top. The apple's circle that contains the pentagram directs our attention to the eternal cycle of life, the ultimate wholeness of all reality.

Several Christian feast days also fall in September. The birthday of Mary, the mother of Jesus, is celebrated on September 8, and the feast day of St. Ninian falls on the sixteenth. Ninian probably lived from about 360 to 432. Little is known for sure about his life, but he is believed to have been the first to bring Christianity to the Picts in southern Scotland. His home base was on the Isle of Whithorn, where he established a religious community, and after his death, he was buried there. St Ninian's Cave, on the shore southwest of Whithorn, has become a place of pilgrimage. The Scots royal family was very devoted to Ninian. In 2010, when the Pope visited Scotland, he did so on St. Ninian's Day, which was celebrated with parades and piping.

Finally, Michaelmas is generally considered to fall on September 29 (though according to some older calendars the date of Michaelmas was October 10). Michael is one of the principal angelic warriors, a protector against evil, important to Celtic Christians. Since Michaelmas is the time when the darker nights and colder days begin, the celebration of Michaelmas is associated with petitions for protection during these dark months. Negative forces were believed to be stronger in darkness, and so families would require stronger defenses during autumn and winter. Traditionally, a well-fattened goose was eaten on Michaelmas to protect against financial need in the family for the next year; according to an old saying, "Eat a goose on Michaelmas Day, want not for money all the year." As a result, Michaelmas was also known as Goose Day, and "goose fairs" were held to celebrate. In Scotland, St, Michael's Bannock is baked in honor of the day by the family's oldest daughter, who repeats, "Progeny and prosperity of family, mystery of Michael, protection of the Trinity." Another traditional chant for Michaelmas speaks of Michaelmas daisies: "The Michaelmas daisies, among dead weeds, bloom for St. Michael's valorous deeds, the last of flowers that stood, till the feast of St. Simon and St. Jude." (The Feast of St. Simon and Jude is at the end of October.) Giving someone a Michaelmas daisy symbolizes saying farewell, in the same way that Michaelmas Day says farewell to the productive year and welcomes in the new cycle of the wheel's year.

Autumn Equinox Ritual

In honor of the equinox, bake an apple cake, using the following recipe:

- ¹/₂ cup butter, softened
- 1 cup sugar
- 2 eggs
- ¹/₄ teaspoon vanilla
- 1 ¹/₄ cups all-purpose flour
- 1 teaspoon baking soda
- 1 teaspoon cinnamon
- ¹/₄ teaspoon salt
- 1 ¹/₂ cups peeled and grated apples
  (about 2 medium apples)
- ¹/₂ cup chopped walnuts

Beat butter, sugar, and eggs until they are fluffy. Stir in vanilla, flour, baking soda, cinnamon, and salt. Add apples and walnuts. Spoon into an 8-inch square pan. Bake 40 to 45 minutes at 350°F. Cake is done when a toothpick inserted in the center comes out clean. Cool 10 minutes, and then remove from pan to cooling rack for another 10 minutes longer. Serve warm with ice cream.

As you make your cake, pray for balance in your life—and as you serve it to friends and family, offer thanks for the abundance of life.

VINE MOON PRAYER

A modern prayer.

In the light of the Vine Moon,
I lie down and rest.
In your name, O Jesu,
I lie down to sleep.
Watch me with Your light;
hold me in Your palm.
May Your moon be a light
to aid me in the dark swamp;
Your light be a shield,
that leads me to life eternal.
Keep me in the presence of God.
I ask that Your light remain with me
from my lying down to my rising.

THE BIRTHDAY OF MARY (SEPTEMBER 8)

Adapted from the Carmina Gadelica.

Mary the fragrant,
Mother of the Shepherd of the flocks,
Hear my prayer as I harvest the new corn.
I will dry it gently in the sun.
I will husk it with my own palms
I will grind it into flour,
and share it with anyone who hungers.

Today I go sunways around my dwelling,
in your name, Mary Mother,
who has preserved me through summer heat,
and will preserve me,
through autumn wind and winter cold,
in peace, in sufficiency,
in work, in love,
in wisdom, in mercy,
for the sake of Your Son,
the Christ of all grace.

Till the day of my death,
do not forsake me!
Till the day of my death,
you will not forsake me!

PRAYER TO ST. NINIAN (SEPTEMBER 16)

A modern prayer.

Blessed Ninian,

we ask that you walk with us

as we, like you,

journey to unknown lands,

places we have not yet explored,

thoughts and ideas that are unfamiliar.

Share with us your courage,

your dedication,

your fidelity and love.

Blessed Ninian,

walk with us.

MABON PRAYER

A modern prayer.

Help us, Mother God,
to find the balance of Mabon.
Teach us that for all that is dark,
there is light;
for all that is bad,
there is good;
for all that causes sorrow,
there is that which causes joy;
and for all that falls,
there is new rising,
each in its time.
May we find Your balance,
Mother God, in our lives,
and in our hearts.
Prepare us for winter's dark.
May we rest in You, unafraid.

PRAYER FOR THE AUTUMN EQUINOX

Modern prayer by Ray Simpson.

O sacred season of autumn, be our teacher,

for we wish to learn the virtue of contentment.

As we gaze upon your full-colored beauty

we sense all about you an at-home-ness

with your amber riches.

You are the season of retirement,

of full barns and harvested fields.

The cycle of growth has ceased

and the busy work of giving life

is now completed.

We sense in you no regrets;

for you have lived a full life.

MICHAELMAS PRAYER (SEPTEMBER 29)

From the Carmina Gadelica.

O Michael the victorious,
I live my life under your shield.
Michael of the white steed,
of the bright brilliant blades,
conqueror of the dragon,
you are at my back,
ranger of the Heavens,
warrior of the Ruler of all.
O Michael the victorious,
be my only pride,
be my guide and the glory of my eye.
I live my life in fellowship with you.
in the meadow, on the mountain,
in summer's last sun and winter's first chill.

Though I should travel the world's hard globe,
no harm can befall me
beneath the shelter of your shield.
O Michael the victorious,
jewel of my heart, God's shepherd,
lead me into ever-peace
with the sacred Three of Glory.

May peace be with my animals,
with the land,
with all plants and trees.
Everything on high or low,
every furnishing or flock,
I give to the holy Triune of glory,
and to you, O Michael the victorious.

MICHAELMAS BLESSING

Adapted from the Carmina Gadelica.

Michael, angel of glory,
bless all things that come together:
all rivers that meet and flow as one;
all milk and eggs and butter
beaten together in the bowl,
all harvest fruit and grain,
in the name of God the Son,
who gave them growth in summer's sun.

There shall be no lack in our house,
for Michael, my love,
has bequeathed to us his power,
with the blessing of the Lamb,
and of His Mother.

On this autumn morn,
I kneel at your footstool, Michael bright warrior.
Be a sanctuary all around me.
Guard me against specter, goblin, and all oppression.
Preserve us and keep us safe.

Consecrate all that we have done this year,
and use it for health and holiness.
Bestow prosperity and peace
to last us through the winter,
in the name of the Creator.

Dandelion and garlic, marigold and onion,
yew and oak and purple heath,
I will bless them all
in the precious name of the Son of God,
in the name of Mary the generous,
and of Patrick,
and of Michael, angel of glory.
O Michael, angel of glory,
bless all things that come together
in harvest time.

Let me not forget when we take our food,
to sprinkle blessing along with salt
in the name of God.
Let me not forget when I bathe the children,
to dip them in the grace of God.

O Michael, angel of glory,
as our barns fill with harvest bounty,
give us truth as heaped and full,
under the strength of Christ always.

SUPPLICATION ON THE NIGHT OF MICHAELMAS

From the Carmina Gadelica.

O Michael, guardian of my right hand,
attend to me this night.
Rescue me from the battling floods of autumn.
Dress me in your linen, for I am naked in the autumn wind
Give me your strength, for I am feeble and forlorn.
Steer my coracle through the crooked eddies,
guide my step over gap and pit.
Guard me in life's treacherous twists,
and save me from all wicked harm.
Save me from harm this night.
Wash from me all taint of pollution.
Encompass me till the Last Day.
O Michael, kind Angel of my right hand,
deliver me from all wickedness this night.
Deliver me this night!

The Ivy Moon

As the Celtic year comes to a close, and Samhain approaches again, the Ivy Moon brings the end of the harvest season. The Celts called this month Gort (pronounced "go-ert"). Ivy often lives on trees, and it can live on after its host plant has died, yet another reminder that life goes on, in the endless cycle of life, death, and rebirth. Ivy is an evergreen plant, and as such it represents eternity and immortality. The ivy is also a strong plant that can grow in the most challenging environments. As the cold months of winter begin, and the wheel of the year comes full circle, the ivy reminds us that the wheel will turn again—and yet again. Life always renews itself.

The Ivy Moon

(OCTOBER)

Although no Pagan holidays fall during the month of October, the third day is the feast day of St. Gwen Teirbron—or Gwen Triple-Breasted. She is thought to have been born in a Welsh community in Brittany, around the turn of the sixth century. She married twice and was the mother of several saints, including St. Cadfan, a Welsh abbot. According to legend, Gwen was twice kidnapped by Anglo Saxon pirates, but each time she escaped by walking on the water of the English Channel in order to return to her home in Britanny. After her children were grown and she was widowed for the second time, she moved to what is now Dorset, where she lived for many years in a small hermitage. Eventually, however, the Saxons ransacked her home and murdered her. A church was built over her grave in Whitchurch, and her shrine still remains there. (She is called St. Wite, since "white" is the English meaning of *Gwen*). She was a popular saint because of God's gift to her of a third breast, and she was invoked by women struggling with infertility and breastfeeding problems. Some scholars speculate that she was the Christianization of a far more ancient fertility goddess.

AUTUMN PRAYER

A modern prayer by Ray Simpson.

As the trees are stripped of foliage
may we be stripped of clutter.
As the leaves fall to the ground
may we fall into your lap.
As the crops ready for harvest are gathered
may the wisdom of our days be garnered.

PRAYER TO ST. GWEN TEIRBRON (OCTOBER 3)

A modern prayer.

Sweet White One,
fertile one, fruitful one,
bless, I pray, my life
with your bounty.
May my life, like yours,
be abundant,
rich with nourishment.
When adversity strikes,
may I, like you, remain faithful
to life's fertility,
its endless plenty.

REAPING BLESSING

Adapted from the Carmina Gadelica.

God, bless my reaping,
each ridge and plain and field;
each sickle I take into my hand,
curved, shapely, hard;
each ear and handful of corn.

Bless each young girl, each boy,
each woman, child, and man.
Safeguard them beneath Your shield of strength,
and guard them in the house of the saints.
Guard them in Your house with all the saints.

Encompass each goat, sheep, and lamb,
each cow, horse, dog, and cat,
and tend them well,
for the sake of Michael, head of Your hosts,
for the sake of Mary, fair-skinned branch of grace,
for the sake of Brigid of fiery spirit.

I give thanks to the God of grace,
for the crops of the ground.
God gives food to us and to our beasts,
enough to last till spring.
James and John, Peter and Paul,
Mary beloved, the fullness of light,
we pray to you
for food to last till spring.

PRAYER FOR GRINDING CORN

A modern prayer.

Brigid of great plenty,
May we have enough to last
until the spring.
We shall have mead,
we shall have wine,
we shall have feast.
we shall have sweetness and milk and cheese,
honey and wholesome ambrosia,
an abundance of that,
an abundance to last
until the spring.
We shall play the harp,
we shall play the lute
and the horn and the strings,
we shall sing and have songs.

Fair Brigid, calm Brigid, be with us.
Gentle Mary Mother, be with us.
Michael, chief of bright blades,
be with us.

Creator of all and Jesus Christ,

and the Spirit of peace,

be with us.

And grace for all,

be with us.

And grace for all,

be with us.

PRAYER FOR SAMHAIN'S EVE

Modern prayer by Ray Simpson.

Star Kindler,

be our light in the darkness that lies ahead.

Weaver of wonder,

weave in us your patterns in the winter that lies ahead.

Gatherer of souls,

encompass those who we see no longer.

Rock of our salvation,

when dark cares loom large be our firm foundation.

We draw near to you.

OCTOBER PRAYER

Adapted from the Carmina Gadelica.

I lie down in the light of the moon,
And God lies down with me.
I lie down with Christ,
And Christ lies down with me.
I lie down with the Spirit,
And the Spirit lies down with me.
In the white light of the moon,
God and Christ and the Spirit
Will lie with me until the sun.
Being of marvels,
Shield me with Your might.
Compass me between earth and sky
In the white light of the moon.

And now we give You thanks
for Your ancient promise
that while the earth endures,
seedtime and harvest, cold and heat,
summer and winter, day and night,
Your love will never cease.

—*Book of Common Prayer*

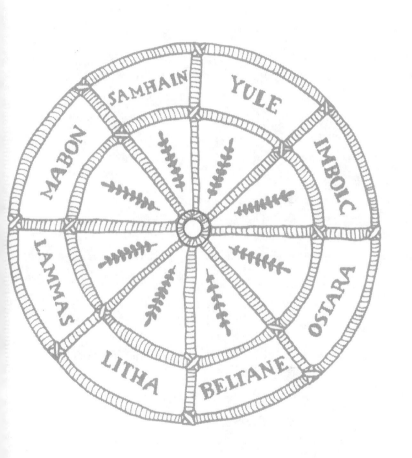

Celtic Prayers for Time of Crisis

Times of crisis test us, physically, emotionally, spiritually. But crises can also be opportunities for change, for renewed health, and new visions. Our response can make all the difference. Will we let crisis defeat us? Or will we rise to the challenge and one day emerge from these catastrophic events as better people building a better world? Change must come; it is inevitable. But the form that change takes is at least partly up to us.

The prayers collected here, written in the Celtic tradition, offer us ways to spiritually meet the crises of our day. They call us to hope and to healing, to blessing others and to receiving strength and courage. They remind us that the Divine One is at work, even now, ever here.

Celtic Prayers
FOR TIMES OF CRISIS

COMPILED BY ELLYN SANNA

Paperback Price: $12.99

Kindle Price: $4.99

Earth Afire with God
Celtic Prayers for Ordinary Life

Here are prayers and blessings to sanctify your daily life. They will remind you to look for the holiness of the everyday; they will show you the real presence of God in Creation.

Kenneth McIntosh, author of Water from an Ancient Well, Celtic Spirituality for Modern Life, writes, "This book knocks the dust off ancient treasures—such as selections from the Carmina Gadelica—and also introduces some lovely new prayers, all written from the Celtic perspective. Earth Afire with God will bless individuals' lives and be equally as useful for small group or worship gatherings."

Illumine your life with the ancient Celts' perspective on prayer. Each glimpse we have of the Earth's beauty, each ordinary sound we hear, every bite of food we eat, and even our daily routines, can all reveal God. This book will help you recognize the everyday revelations that surround you.

Paperback Price: $12.99

Kindle Price: $4.99

Tree of Life

Celtic Prayers to the Universal Christ

Christ is the visible image of the invisible God.
He existed before anything was created and is supreme over all
creation, for through him God created everything. . . .
He existed before anything else, and he holds all creation together.
—Colossians 1:15–17

Like a vast, ever-growing Tree of Life, Christ—the expression of Divine love—expands endlessly throughout the universe. This is the perspective of ancient Celtic spirituality, and it is this concept that Ray Simpson reveals in his poem-prayers. Inspired by the traditional Celtic style of prayer, he gives words to our individual

relationships with God. He speaks of the wonder, beauty, and love revealed through the Universal Christ, the Tree of Life that includes all that is. Each and everything in creation is sacred, for everything is a word of God—and we too are called to be God's words to our world.

Paperback Price: $19.99

Kindle Price: $5.99

The Celtic Book of Days

Ancient Wisdom for Each Day of the Year from the Celtic Followers of Christ

This book will change the way you look at everyday life.

The ancient Celts found God's presence in each ordinary moment of the day. Everything they encountered revealed to them the presence of the sacred; each day was deep with meaning. Now you too can practice the Celts' faith, as you take a few moments to immerse yourself in their wisdom. These small daily moments of reflection and insight will open your heart to each day and all it holds.

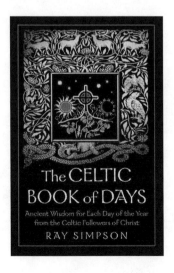

Paperback Price: $28.99

Kindle Price: $9.99

AnamcharaBooks.com

Made in the USA
Las Vegas, NV
12 August 2023